WITH ONE VOICE

A Lutheran Resource for Worship

Leaders Edition

Augsburg Fortress
Minneapolis

WITH ONE VOICE
A Lutheran Resource for Worship

Leaders Edition

Also available:
Pew Edition (3-301)
Accompaniment Edition (3-302)
Instrumental Parts (3-304)
Cassette Recording of the Liturgies (3-305)

The paper used in this publication meets the minimum requirements of American National Standards for Information Sciences—Permanence of Paper for Printed Library Materials, ANSI Z329.48-1984.

Manufactured in the U.S.A.   ISBN 0-8066-0138-8   AF 3-303

03 02 01 00 99 98   5 6 7 8 9 10 11 12 13 14 15

CONTENTS

INTRODUCTION

With One Voice has been prepared as an additional volume of resources for Lutherans at worship. It is intended to stand beside the principal worship book presently in use and to supplement its contents.

Several premises underlie the preparation of this collection. *With One Voice* is oriented primarily to the principal weekly assembly of God's people. These new liturgical settings, hymns, and songs are offered to assist those who gather around the Word and Sacraments, and to support the lectionary as it unfolds the saving story through the seasons of the Christian year.

The title suggests another focus of the volume. The letter to the Romans contains the exhortation to "live in harmony with one another…that together you may with one voice glorify…God" (Romans 15:5–6). A quick glance at this resource will reveal that to sing "with one voice" does not imply uniformity of expression. The "one voice" of the Church represents an amazingly diverse fabric, many songs of many cultures in many styles, woven together by the one Spirit. The size of *With One Voice* allows only a sampling of these many songs, but the breadth represented here is a witness to the Church's unity in diversity and an encouragement to communities to cultivate a variety of expressions when they gather, rather than dividing themselves by style of worship or music.

The liturgy of Holy Communion in *With One Voice* continues to "embody the tradition of worship which received its characteristic shape during the early centuries of the Church's existence and was reaffirmed during the Reformation era" (Introduction, *Lutheran Book of Worship*). The design of the services in this volume aims to reveal this characteristic shape. Two services of Holy Communion (*Light of Christ* and *Bread of Life*) are presented with complete musical settings. Holy Communion: *All Times and Places,* Setting 6, follows the model of Martin Luther's Chorale Service and suggests the insertion of service music from a wide variety of sources to be used for the principal musical elements. It is a flexible structure enabling the celebration of Holy Communion with integrity while allowing for adaptation to various circumstances.

This resource includes also a Service of Word and Prayer, incorporating service music, proclamation of the Word, creed and confession, offering and prayer.

The many songs gathered together in the hymn collection of *With One Voice* include a large number that have already found their way into the repertoire of many Lutheran assemblies. In addition to well-loved hymns from several traditions, there are contributions from the diverse cultures of North America as well as a representative sampling of materials from other parts of the world. Songs that center around a repeated refrain (choruses, materials from Taizé) stand alongside the lively poetry and new melodies of the "hymnic explosion" of the last two decades. Strong and singable melodies have been prized in every genre represented. Accompaniments are included throughout for the hymns and songs in order to enable the use of these materials in a variety of settings and to enable singing in harmony where appropriate.

Throughout this supplementary resource careful attention has been given to the use of language that includes all God's people and employs a broadened palette of images for the persons of the Trinity. Liturgical texts are in continuity with those prepared for *LBW*, incorporating several further revisions of the English Language Liturgical Consultation (an ecumenical group representing major English-speaking churches) published in *Praying Together* (1988). The ELLC versions of the Apostles' and Nicene Creeds are provided on pages 54–55, and congregations are encouraged to study them for possible use.

Thirty years ago, Lutherans in North America entered into a significant process in the development of common worship resources as the Inter-Lutheran Commission on Worship undertook work leading toward a renewal in the worship life of the Lutheran churches. In the intervening years, the rapid change of contemporary society has confronted the world and the Church. While the fundamental pattern of the Church's worship does not change, the ways that Christians at worship express themselves in word, music, and gesture are always unfolding. Developed by the Publishing House and the Division for Congregational Ministries of the Evangelical Lutheran Church in America, with consultation and review provided by congregations and lay persons, church musicians and pastors, theologians and ecumenical partners, *With One Voice* is offered as a further vehicle for the richly varied and constantly emerging praise and prayer of the Church.

May *With One Voice* be a useful instrument so that "joined together in harmony and having received the godly melody in unison, you might sing in one voice through Jesus Christ…that you might always partake of God."

(Ephesians IV, Ignatius of Antioch, c. 35–c. 107 A.D.)

> It is the voice of the Church that is heard in singing together.
> It is not you that sings, it is the Church that is singing,
> and you, as a member of the Church, may share in its song.
> Thus all singing together…serves to widen our spiritual horizon,
> make us see our little company as a member
> of the great Christian Church on earth,
> and help us willingly and gladly to join our singing,
> be it feeble or good,
> to the song of the Church.
> Dietrich Bonhöffer, *Life Together*

In addition to the Leaders Edition, an Accompaniment Edition with complete liturgical music and the entire collection of hymns and songs with additional alternate harmonizations is available, as well as a Pew Edition, which contains materials needed by the Christian assembly. All three editions are necessary in order for *With One Voice* to be used to its full potential.

FOUNDATIONS FOR THE CHRISTIAN ASSEMBLY

From the earliest days of the Church, Christian worship has been marked by a pattern of gathering, word, meal, and sending. These basic elements—revealed in the New Testament, the writings of the early Church, the Lutheran confessions, and ecumenical documents—constitute the center of the Church's worship.

Beginning with Moses and all the prophets, Jesus interpreted to them the things about himself in all the scriptures. ... When he was at table with them, he took bread, blessed and broke it, and gave it to them. Then their eyes were opened and they recognized him.

Luke 24:27, 30–31a

The baptized devoted themselves to the apostles' teaching and fellowship, to the breaking of bread and the prayers.

Acts 2:42

On Sunday all are gathered together in unity. The records of the apostles or the writings of the prophets are read for as long as time allows. The presider exhorts and invites us into the pattern of these good things. Then we all stand and offer prayer.

When we have concluded the prayer, bread is set out together with wine. ... The presider then offers prayer and thanksgiving and the people sing out their assent, saying the "Amen." There is a distribution of the things over which thanks has been said and each person participates, and these things are sent to those who are not present.

Those who are prosperous give what they wish according to each one's own choice, and the collection is deposited with the presider, who aids orphans and widows, those in want because of disease, those in prison, and foreigners who are staying here.

We hold this meeting together on Sunday since it is the first day, on which God, having transformed darkness and matter, created the world. On the same day Jesus Christ our Savior rose from the dead. On Sunday he appeared to his apostles and disciples and taught them these things which we present to you.

From the Apology of Justin Martyr (c. 150 A.D.)

It is taught among us that one holy Christian church will be and remain forever. This is the assembly of all believers among whom the Gospel is preached in its purity and the holy sacraments are administered according to the Gospel.

For it is sufficient for the true unity of the Christian church that the Gospel be preached in conformity with a pure understanding of it and that the sacraments be administered in accordance with the divine Word. It is not necessary for the true unity of the Christian church that humanly instituted ceremonies should be observed uniformly in all places.

Augsburg Confession VII (1530)

The Church earnestly desires that all the faithful be led to that full, conscious, and active participation in liturgical celebrations called for by the very nature of the liturgy. Such participation by the Christian people as "a chosen race, a royal priesthood, a holy nation, God's own people" (1 Peter 2:9; see 2:4–5) is their right and duty by reason of their baptism.

Constitution on the Liturgy, Second Vatican Council (1963)

The services of *Lutheran Book of Worship* embody the tradition of worship which received its characteristic shape during the early centuries of the Church's existence and was reaffirmed during the Reformation era. ...

Freedom and flexibility in worship is a Lutheran inheritance, and there is room for ample variety in ceremony, music, and liturgical form. Having considered their resources and their customs, congregations will find their own balance between fully using the ritual and musical possibilities of the liturgy, and a more modest practice. A full service should not allow secondary ceremonies to eclipse central elements of the liturgy, nor should a simple service omit essential or important parts.

Every service, whether elaborate or spare, sung or said, should be within the framework of the common rite of the Church, so that the integrity of the rite is always respected and maintained.

Lutheran Book of Worship (1978)

HOLY COMMUNION
Shape of the Rite

Sunday is the primary day on which the Church assembles: the first day of creation when God transformed darkness into light and the day on which Christ rose from death and revealed himself to the disciples in the scriptures and the breaking of the bread. The baptized gather to hear the word, to pray for those in need, to offer thanks to God for the gift of salvation, to receive the bread of life and the cup of blessing, and to be renewed for the daily witness of faith, hope, and love. To guests, strangers, and all in need, the Church offers these good things of God's grace.

GATHERING

Entrance Hymn
GREETING
Kyrie
Hymn of Praise
PRAYER OF THE DAY

God calls and gathers believers through the Holy Spirit, and in response the community acclaims this gracious God in song and prayer. The gathering of the congregation may begin with a confession of sin and/or an entrance hymn. God's welcome is extended to the congregation by the presider. When appropriate, a litany or hymn of praise may be sung immediately before the prayer of the day. Through these actions, the congregation prepares to hear the Word of God.

WORD

FIRST READING
Psalm
Second Reading
Gospel Acclamation
GOSPEL
SERMON
HYMN OF THE DAY
Creed
THE PRAYERS

In the rich treasure of Scripture proclaimed by readers and preachers, the Church hears the good news of God acting in this and every time and place. A three-year cycle of readings provides portions of the Hebrew Scriptures, the New Testament letters, and the Gospel books for each week. During Advent/Christmas, the lectionary reveals the mystery of the Word made flesh. In Lent/Easter, the paschal mystery of the Lord's death and resurrection is proclaimed. Throughout the Season after Pentecost, the New Testament texts are read in a continuous order. During the last Sundays of the year, the readings present the final vision of a new heaven and a new earth.

This encounter with the living Word, Jesus Christ, is marked by proclamation and silence, psalm and hymn, singing and speaking, movement and gesture. Silence after the readings allows time for the word to be pondered. The sermon announces good news for the community and the world; the hymn of the day both proclaims and responds to the word; a creed is a further response to it. God's Word, read and preached and acclaimed, leads the community to pray for the Church, the people of the world, and those who suffer or are in need.

MEAL

Greeting of Peace
PRESENTATION OF THE GIFTS
GREAT THANKSGIVING
LORD'S PRAYER
COMMUNION
Canticle
Prayer

In thanksgiving, the congregation praises God for the gracious gifts of creation and the saving deeds of Jesus Christ. To the table of the Lord are brought bread and wine, simple signs of God's love, humble signs of human labor. In word and gesture, prayer and song, the people lift up their hearts in praise and thanksgiving for the gifts of forgiveness, life, and salvation, hearing Jesus' words spoken at this supper, remembering his death and resurrection. The presider asks that the Holy Spirit unite the community in the Lord's bread and cup so that, as one body in Christ, it too might proclaim God's salvation in the world. To this grateful proclamation, the community joins its "Amen" before praying the Lord's Prayer with one voice. Welcomed to the table, each one is united with God in Christ, with each other, and with the Church's mission in the world. During the communion, hymns, songs, and psalms may be sung. As the table is cleared, the congregation may sing a canticle. A brief prayer concludes the liturgy of the meal.

SENDING

BLESSING
Dismissal

Worship on the Lord's Day ends with simplicity. The community receives the blessing of God. All are invited to leave in peace, sent out to serve in word and deed: to speak the words of good news they have heard, to care for those in need, and to share what they have received with the poor and the hungry.

Central elements of the Holy Communion liturgy are noted in uppercase letters; other elements support and reveal the essential shape of Christian worship.

BRIEF ORDER FOR CONFESSION AND FORGIVENESS

Stand

The minister leads the congregation in the invocation. The sign of the cross may be made by all in remembrance of their Baptism.

P In the name of the Father, and of the ✛ Son, and of the Holy Spirit.

C **Amen**

The minister continues, using one of the sections below.

OR

P Almighty God,
to whom all hearts are open,
all desires known,
and from whom no secrets are hid:
Cleanse the thoughts of our hearts
by the inspiration of your Holy Spirit,
that we may perfectly love you
and worthily magnify your holy name,
through Jesus Christ our Lord. (236)

C **Amen**

P God of all mercy and consolation,
come to the aid of your people,
turning us from our sin
to live for you alone.
Give us the power of your Holy Spirit
that, attentive to your Word,
we may confess our sins,
receive your forgiveness,
and grow into the fullness of your Son,
Jesus Christ our Lord. (574)

C **Amen**

P If we say we have no sin,
we deceive ourselves,
and the truth is not in us.
But if we confess our sins,
God who is faithful and just
will forgive our sins
and cleanse us from all unrighteousness.

P Let us confess our sin in the
presence of God and of one another.

Kneel/Stand

Silence for reflection and self-examination.

℗ Most merciful God,
☾ **we confess
that we are in bondage to sin
and cannot free ourselves.
We have sinned against you
in thought, word, and deed,
by what we have done
and by what we have left undone.
We have not loved you
with our whole heart;
we have not loved
our neighbors as ourselves.
For the sake of your Son, Jesus Christ,
have mercy on us.
Forgive us, renew us, and lead us,
so that we may delight in your will
and walk in your ways,
to the glory of your holy name. Amen**

℗ Gracious God,
☾ **have mercy on us.
In your compassion
forgive us our sins,
known and unknown,
things done and left undone.
Uphold us by your Spirit
so that we may live and serve you
in newness of life,
to the honor and glory of your holy name;
through Jesus Christ our Lord. Amen**

The minister stands and addresses the congregation.

℗ In the mercy of almighty God,
Jesus Christ was given to die for us,
and for his sake
God forgives us all our sins.
As a called and ordained minister of the
Church of Christ, and by his authority,
I therefore declare to you
the entire forgiveness of all your sins,
in the name of the Father,
and of the ✝ Son, and of the Holy Spirit.
☾ **Amen**

℗ Almighty God have mercy on you,
forgive you all your sins
through our Lord Jesus Christ,
strengthen you in all goodness,
and by the power of the Holy Spirit
keep you in eternal life.
☾ **Amen**

HOLY COMMUNION
Light of Christ, Setting 4

The Brief Order for Confession and Forgiveness (p. 10) may be used before this service.
The minister may announce the day and its significance before the Entrance Hymn or before the readings.

GATHERING

Stand

ENTRANCE HYMN or Psalm

GREETING

The minister greets the congregation.

Ⓟ The grace of our Lord Jesus Christ, the love of God,
and the communion of the Holy Spirit be with you all.
Ⓒ **And also with you.**

KYRIE

The Kyrie may follow.

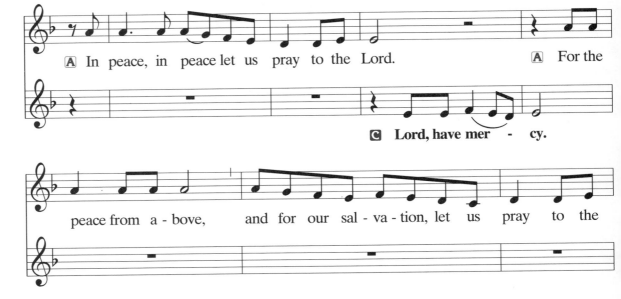

Ⓐ In peace, in peace let us pray to the Lord.   Ⓐ For the

Ⓒ Lord, have mer - cy.

peace from a - bove,   and for our sal - va - tion, let us pray to the

Lord.

A For the peace of the whole world, the well-be-ing of the

C Lord, have mer - cy.

Church of God, and for the u-ni-ty of all, let us pray to the

Lord.

A For this ho-ly house, and for all who of-fer here their

C Lord, have mer - cy.

wor-ship and praise, let us pray to the Lord.

C Lord, have mer - cy.

A Help, save, com-fort, and de-fend us, gra-cious Lord.

C A - men

HYMN OF PRAISE

The Hymn of Praise or another appropriate hymn may be sung.

C Glo-ry to God in the high - est, and peace to God's peo-ple on earth.

1 Lord God, heav-en-ly king, al-might-y God and Fa-ther, we
wor-ship you, we give you thanks, we praise you for your glo - ry.

2 Lord Je - sus Christ, on - ly Son of the Fa - ther,
Lord God, Lamb of God, you take a - way the sin of the
world: have mer - cy, have mer-cy on us; you are seat - ed
at the right hand of the Fa - ther: re - ceive our prayer.

3 For you a - lone are the Ho - ly One, you a - lone are the Lord,
you a - lone are the Most High, Je - sus Christ, with the Ho - ly Spir-it,
in the glo - ry of God the Fa - ther. A - men.

The Prayer of the Day follows on page 16.

OR

This is the feast of vic - to - ry for our God.

Al - le - lu - ia, al - le - lu - ia.

I Wor - thy is Christ, the Lamb who was slain, whose

blood set us free to be peo - ple of God.

II Pow - er and rich - es, wis - dom and strength, and

hon - or and bless - ing and glo - ry are his.

This is the feast of vic - to - ry for our God.

Al - le - lu - ia, al - le - lu - ia.

I Sing with all the peo - ple of God, and

join in the hymn of all cre - a - tion:

Ⅱ Bless - ing and hon - or, glo - ry and might to God and the

Lamb for - ev - er. A - men

C This is the feast of vic - to - ry for our God.

Al - le - lu - ia, al - le - lu - ia.

Ⅰ Ⅱ For the Lamb, the Lamb who was slain has be -

gun his reign. Al - le - lu - ia.

C This is the feast of vic - to - ry for our God. Al - le -

lu - ia, al - le - lu - ia, al - le - lu - ia. A - men

PRAYER OF THE DAY

The salutation may precede the prayer.

Ⓟ The Lord be with you.
C And also with you.

Ⓟ Let us pray. *(The Prayer of the Day is said, concluding:)*
C Amen

WORD

Sit

FIRST READING

🅐 A reading from _____.

After the reading, the reader may say: The word of the Lord.
All may respond: **Thanks be to God.**

PSALM

The Psalm is sung or said.

SECOND READING

🅐 A reading from _____.

After the reading, the reader may say: The word of the Lord.
All may respond: **Thanks be to God.**

Stand

GOSPEL ACCLAMATION

The appointed Verse may be sung by the choir, or the congregation may sing a general acclamation or a hymn.

GENERAL

LENT

GOSPEL

The Gospel is announced.

Ⓟ The Holy Gospel according to _____, the _____ chapter.

Ⓒ **Glory to you, O Lord.**

After the reading:

Ⓟ The Gospel of the Lord.

Ⓒ **Praise to you, O Christ.**

Sit

SERMON

Silence for reflection may follow.

Stand

HYMN OF THE DAY

CREED

A Creed may be said: the Nicene Creed, on all festivals and on Sundays in the seasons of Advent/Christmas and Lent/Easter; the Apostles' Creed, at other times. When Holy Baptism or another rite with a creed is celebrated, this creed may be omitted.

NICENE CREED

Ⓒ **We believe in one God,**
    the Father, the Almighty,
    maker of heaven and earth,
    of all that is, seen and unseen.

  We believe in one Lord, Jesus Christ,
    the only Son of God,
    eternally begotten of the Father,
    God from God, Light from Light,
    true God from true God,
    begotten, not made,
    of one Being with the Father.
    Through him all things were made.
    For us and for our salvation
      he came down from heaven;
      by the power of the Holy Spirit
        he became incarnate from the virgin Mary, and was made man.

For our sake he was crucified under Pontius Pilate;
    he suffered death and was buried.
    On the third day he rose again
        in accordance with the Scriptures;
    he ascended into heaven
        and is seated at the right hand of the Father.
He will come again in glory to judge the living and the dead,
    and his kingdom will have no end.

We believe in the Holy Spirit, the Lord, the giver of life,
    who proceeds from the Father and the Son.
    With the Father and the Son he is worshiped and glorified.
    He has spoken through the prophets.
    We believe in one holy catholic and apostolic Church.
    We acknowledge one Baptism for the forgiveness of sins.
    We look for the resurrection of the dead,
        and the life of the world to come. Amen

APOSTLES' CREED

C I believe in God, the Father almighty,
    creator of heaven and earth.

I believe in Jesus Christ, his only Son, our Lord.
    He was conceived by the power of the Holy Spirit
        and born of the virgin Mary.
    He suffered under Pontius Pilate,
        was crucified, died, and was buried.
    He descended into hell.*
    On the third day he rose again.
    He ascended into heaven,
        and is seated at the right hand of the Father.
    He will come again to judge the living and the dead.

I believe in the Holy Spirit,
    the holy catholic Church,
    the communion of saints,
    the forgiveness of sins,
    the resurrection of the body,
    and the life everlasting. Amen

*Or, He descended to the dead.

Stand/Kneel

THE PRAYERS

The Prayers begin with these or similar words:

Ⓐ Let us pray for the whole people of God in Christ Jesus,
and for all people according to their needs.

Prayers are included for the whole Church, the nations, those in need, the parish, and special concerns. The congregation may be invited to offer other petitions. The minister gives thanks for the faithful departed, especially for those who recently have died.

Each portion of the prayers concludes with these or similar words:

	OR
Ⓐ Lord, in your mercy,	Ⓐ Hear us, O God;
Ⓒ **hear our prayer.**	Ⓒ **your mercy is great.**

The prayers conclude with these or similar words:

Ⓟ Into your hands, O Lord, we commend all for whom we pray,
trusting in your mercy; through your Son, Jesus Christ our Lord.
Ⓒ **Amen**

MEAL

Stand

PEACE

The Peace is shared.

Ⓟ The peace of the Lord be with you always.
Ⓒ **And also with you.**

The ministers and congregation may greet one another with a gesture of peace, using these or similar words: **Peace be with you.**

Sit

PRESENTATION OF THE GIFTS

The Offering is received as the Lord's Table is prepared.

The appointed Offertory may be sung by the choir as the gifts are presented, or the congregation may sing the following offertory, or an appropriate hymn or psalm may be sung.

Stand

C Let the vine-yards be fruit-ful, Lord, fill to the brim our cup of bless-ing. Gath-er a har-vest from the seeds that were sown, that we may be fed, we may be fed with the bread of life. Gath-er the hopes and the dreams of all; u-nite them with the prayers we of-fer now. Grace our ta-ble with your pres-ence, and give us a fore-taste of the feast to come.

After the gifts have been presented, one of these prayers or another offertory prayer is said.

A Let us pray.

A Blessed are you,

C **O Lord our God,
maker of all things.
Through your goodness
you have blessed us with these gifts.
With them we offer ourselves
to your service
and dedicate our lives
to the care and redemption
of all that you have made,
for the sake of him
who gave himself for us,
Jesus Christ our Lord. Amen** (240)

OR

A Let us pray.

A Merciful God,

C **we offer with joy and thanksgiving
what you have first given us—
our selves,
our time,
and our possessions,
signs of your gracious love.
Receive them
for the sake of him
who offered himself for us,
Jesus Christ our Lord. Amen** (239)

GREAT THANKSGIVING

The Great Thanksgiving is begun by the presiding minister.

P The Lord be with you.

P Lift up your hearts.

C And al-so with you.

C We lift them to the Lord.

P Let us give thanks to the Lord our God.

C It is right to give our thanks and praise.

P It is indeed right and salutary

that we should at all times and in all places offer thanks and praise to you,

Common
O Lord, holy Father,   through Christ our Lord.
                                                Lord;

Advent, Easter, Holy Trinity, Marriage
O Lord, holy Father, almighty and ev -   er - liv - ing God.

Apostles
O Lord, holy Father,
    through the great shepherd of your   flock, Christ our Lord.

Advent
You comforted your people with the promise of the Redeemer,

Christmas
In the wonder and mystery of the Word made flesh
  you have opened the eyes of faith to a new and radiant vision of your glory;

Epiphany
Sharing our life, he lived among us

Lent
You bid your people cleanse their hearts and prepare with joy
  for the paschal feast.

Passion (I)
who on the tree of the cross gave salvation to all,

Passion (II)
For our sins he was lifted high upon the cross,
  that he might draw the whole world to himself;

Easter
But chiefly we are bound to praise you for the glorious resurrection of our Lord;

Ascension
who, after his resurrection, appeared openly to his disciples

Pentecost
who rose beyond the bounds of death,

Holy Trinity
You have revealed your glory as the glory also of your Son and of the Holy Spirit:

Sundays after Pentecost
who on this day overcame death and the grave,

All Saints
In the blessedness of your saints
  you have given us a glorious pledge of the hope of our calling;

Christ the King
Born as king in David's line,
  his power was revealed in weakness, his majesty in mercy.

Apostles
who after his resurrection sent forth his apostles
  to preach the Gospel and teach all nations,

Baptism
In him you have received us as your children,

Marriage
For your love is firm as the ancient earth, your faithfulness fixed as the heavens.

Burial
who brought to light the living hope of a blessed resurrection,

Advent
through whom you will also make all things new in the day when he comes again

Christmas
that, beholding the God made visible,

Epiphany
to reveal your glory and love,

Lent
Renew our zeal in faith and life, and bring us to the fullness of grace

Passion (I)
that, where death began, there life might be restored,
    and that he, who by a tree once overcame,

Passion (II)
and, by his suffering and death, he became the source of eternal salvation

Easter
for he is the true Passover Lamb who gave himself to take away our sin,
    who by his death has destroyed death,

Ascension
and, in their sight, was taken up into heaven,

Pentecost
and, [on this day,] as he had promised,
    poured out your Spirit of life and power upon the chosen disciples.

Holy Trinity
three persons, equal in majesty, undivided in splendor, yet one Lord, one God,

Sundays after Pentecost
and by his glorious resurrection

All Saints
that, moved by their witness and supported by their fellowship,
    we may run with perseverance the race that is set before us

Christ the King
Once enthroned upon the cross, you raised him from death to your right hand,

Apostles
and promised to be with them always,

Baptism
made us citizens of your kingdom,

Marriage
Creating and enriching and continuing life, you created us male and female
    to fulfill one another; you gave us the gift of marriage which embodies your
    love and which, even where your name is not known,

Burial
that, in our grief, we may rejoice in full assurance of our change

Advent
to judge the world in | righ - teous -ness.

Christmas
we may be drawn to love the God whom we | can - not see.

Epiphany
that our darkness should give way to his own | bril - liant light.

Lent
that belongs to the chil- | dren of God.

Passion (I)
might by a tree be | o - ver - come.

Passion (II)
for all who put their | trust in him.

Easter
and by his rising has brought us to e- | ter - nal life.

Ascension
that he might make us partakers of his divine | na - ture.

Pentecost
At this the whole earth exults in | bound - less joy.

Holy Trinity
ever to be adored in your everlasting | glo - ry.

Sundays after Pentecost
opened to us the way of ever- | last - ing life.

All Saints
and with them receive the unfading crown of | glo - ry.

Christ the King
there to rule forever in your kingdom of justice, | love, and peace.

Apostles
even to the end | of the age.

Baptism
and given us your Holy Spirit to guide us into | all . . . truth.

Marriage
proclaims your love for the whole human | fam - i - ly.

Burial
into the likeness of his | glo - ry.

Common
And so, with the Church on earth and the   hosts of heaven,

Easter
And so, with Mary Magdalene and Peter
    and all the witnesses of the resurrection,
    with earth and sea and all their creatures,
    and with angels and archangels,   cherubim and seraphim,

Apostles
And so, with patriarchs and prophets,
    with the apostle(s) _____,
    and with all the   company of heaven,

we praise your name and join their un - end - ing hymn:

C Ho - ly, ho - ly, ho - ly Lord,

Lord God of pow'r and might, heav-en and earth are

full of your glo - ry. Ho - san - na in the high - est.

Bless - ed, bless - ed is he who comes in the name of the

Lord. Ho - san - na in the high - est.

The minister continues, using one of the prayers below.

℗ You are indeed holy, O God,
   the fountain of all holiness;
   you bring light from darkness,
   life from death,
   speech from silence.

We worship you for our lives
   and for the world you give us.
We thank you
   for the new world to come
   and for the love
   that will rule all in all.
We praise you for the grace
   shown to Israel, your chosen,
   the people of your promise:
   the rescue from Egypt,
   the gift of the promised land,
   the memory of the ancestors,
   the homecoming from exile,
   and the prophets' words
   that will not be in vain.

In all this we bless you
   for your only-begotten Son,
   who fulfilled and will fulfill
   all your promises.

In the night in which he was betrayed,
   our Lord Jesus took bread,
   and gave thanks; broke it,
   and gave it to his disciples,
   saying: Take and eat;
   this is my body, given for you.
Do this for the remembrance of me.

Again, after supper,
   he took the cup, gave thanks,
   and gave it for all to drink,
   saying: This cup is
   the new covenant in my blood,
   shed for you and for all people
   for the forgiveness of sin.
Do this for the remembrance of me.

This prayer continues on page 24.

OR

℗ Holy, mighty, and merciful Lord,
   heaven and earth are full of your glory.

In great love you sent to us Jesus,
   your Son, who reached out
   to heal the sick and suffering,
   who preached good news to the poor,
   and who, on the cross,
   opened his arms to all.

In the night in which he was betrayed,
   our Lord Jesus took bread,
   and gave thanks; broke it,
   and gave it to his disciples,
   saying: Take and eat;
   this is my body, given for you.
Do this for the remembrance of me.

Again, after supper,
   he took the cup, gave thanks,
   and gave it for all to drink,
   saying: This cup is
   the new covenant in my blood,
   shed for you and for all people
   for the forgiveness of sin.
Do this for the remembrance of me.

Remembering, therefore,
   his death, resurrection, and ascension,
   we await his coming in glory.

Pour out your Holy Spirit,
   that by this Holy Communion
   we may know the unity
   we share with all your people
   in the body of your Son,
   Jesus Christ our Lord.

Through him, with him, in him,
   in the unity of the Holy Spirit,
   all glory and honor is yours,
   almighty Father, now and forever.
⬛ **Amen**

The Lord's Prayer follows on page 25.

℗ For as often as we eat of this bread and drink from this cup,
we proclaim the Lord's death until he comes.

C Christ has died. Christ is ris - en.

Christ will come a - gain.

℗ Therefore, O God, with this bread and cup
    we remember the incarnation of your Son:
      his human birth and the covenant he made with us.
We remember the sacrifice of his life:
    his eating with outcasts and sinners,
    and his acceptance of death.
But chiefly we remember his rising from the tomb,
    his ascension to the seat of power,
    and his sending of the holy and life-giving Spirit.
We cry out for the resurrection of our lives,
    when Christ will come again in beauty and power
    to share with us the great and promised feast.

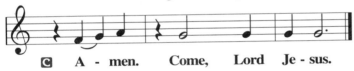

C A - men. Come, Lord Je - sus.

℗ Send now, we pray, your Holy Spirit,
    that we and all who share in this bread and cup
    may be united in the communion of the Holy Spirit,
    may enter the fullness of the kingdom of heaven,
    and may receive our inheritance with all your saints in light.

C A - men. Come, Ho - ly Spir - it.

℗ Join our prayers with those of your servants
    of every time and every place, and unite them
    with the ceaseless petitions of our great high priest
    until he comes as victorious Lord of all.
Through him, with him, in him, in the unity of the Holy Spirit,
    all glory and honor is yours, almighty Father, now and forever.

C A - men, a - men, a - men.

LORD'S PRAYER

P Let us pray with confidence
in the words our Savior gave us:

C **Our Father in heaven,**
   hallowed be your name,
   your kingdom come,
   your will be done,
      on earth as in heaven.
   Give us today our daily bread.
   Forgive us our sins
      as we forgive those
         who sin against us.
   Save us from the time of trial
      and deliver us from evil.
   For the kingdom, the power,
      and the glory are yours,
         now and for ever. Amen

P Lord, remember us in your
kingdom, and teach us to pray:

C **Our Father, who art in heaven,**
   hallowed be thy name,
   thy kingdom come,
   thy will be done,
      on earth as it is in heaven.
   Give us this day our daily bread;
   and forgive us our trespasses,
      as we forgive those
         who trespass against us;
   and lead us not into temptation,
      but deliver us from evil.
   For thine is the kingdom,
      and the power, and the glory,
         forever and ever. Amen

Sit
COMMUNION

The communion follows. The bread may be broken for distribution.
As the ministers give the bread and cup to each communicant, they say these words:
The body of Christ, given for you. The blood of Christ, shed for you.
The communicant may say: **Amen**
As the people commune, hymns and other music may be used, and may include the following:

C Lamb of God, you take a-way the sin of the world;
have mer-cy on us, have mer-cy on us, have mer-cy.
Lamb of God, you take a-way the sin of the world;
have mer-cy on us, have mer-cy on us, have mer-cy.
Lamb of God, you take a-way the sin of the world; grant us peace.

After all have returned to their places, the minister may say these or similar words.

Ⓟ The body and blood of our Lord Jesus Christ strengthen you
and keep you in his grace.

Ⓒ **Amen**

CANTICLE

A post-communion canticle or an appropriate hymn or song may be sung.

Ⓒ Now, Lord, you let your ser - vant go in peace:
your word has been ful - filled. My own eyes have
seen the sal - va - tion which you have pre - pared in the sight of all
peo - ple: a light to re - veal you to the
na - tions and the glo - ry of your peo - ple Is - ra - el.
Glo - ry to the Fa - ther and to the Son, glo - ry to the
Ho - ly Spir - it, as it was in the be - gin - ning, is now, and
will be for - ev - er. A - men, a - men, a - men.

OR

Thank-ful hearts and voic - es raise; tell ev - 'ry - one what God has done. Let all who seek the Lord re - joice, re - joice and bear Christ's ho - ly name. Send us, O God, with your prom - is - es, and lead us forth in joy with shouts of thanks - giv - ing. Al - le - lu - ia, al - le - lu - ia.

PRAYER

The following or a similar post-communion prayer is said.

Ⓐ Let us pray.
Ⓐ Pour out upon us the spirit of your love, O Lord, and unite the wills of those whom you have fed with one heavenly food; through Jesus Christ our Lord. (242)
Ⓒ **Amen**

Silence for reflection.

SENDING

BLESSING

The minister blesses the congregation, using this or another appropriate blessing.

Ⓟ Almighty God, Father, ✙ Son, and Holy Spirit, bless you now and forever.
Ⓒ **Amen**

When there is a procession from the church, a hymn, song, or canticle may be sung.

DISMISSAL

The minister may dismiss the congregation.

Ⓐ Go in peace. Serve the Lord.
Ⓒ **Thanks be to God.**

HOLY COMMUNION
Bread of Life, Setting 5

The Brief Order for Confession and Forgiveness (p. 10) may be used before this service. The minister may announce the day and its significance before the Entrance Hymn or before the readings.

GATHERING

Stand

ENTRANCE HYMN or Psalm

GREETING

The minister greets the congregation.

P The grace of our Lord Jesus Christ, the love of God, and the communion of the Holy Spirit be with you all.

C **And also with you.**

KYRIE

The Kyrie may follow.

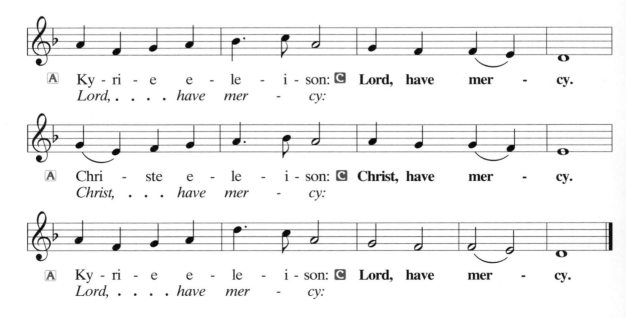

A Ky - ri - e e - le - i - son: C **Lord, have mer - cy.**
Lord, ... have mer - cy:

A Chri - ste e - le - i - son: C **Christ, have mer - cy.**
Christ, . . . have mer - cy:

A Ky - ri - e e - le - i - son: C **Lord, have mer - cy.**
Lord, . . . have mer - cy:

HYMN OF PRAISE

The Hymn of Praise or another appropriate hymn may be sung.

C Glo-ry to God, glo-ry to God, glo-ry to God in the high-est;

glo-ry to God, glo-ry to God, and peace to God's peo-ple on earth.

I Lord God, heav-en-ly king, al-might-y God and Fa-ther, we

wor-ship you, we give you thanks, we praise you for your glo-ry.

C Glo-ry to God, glo-ry to God, glo-ry to God in the high-est;

glo-ry to God, glo-ry to God, and peace to God's peo-ple on earth.

II Lord Je-sus Christ, on-ly Son of the Fa-ther,

Lord God, Lamb of God, you take a-way the sin of the

world: have mer-cy on us; you are seat-ed at the

right hand of the Fa-ther: re-ceive our prayer.

C Glo-ry to God, glo-ry to God, glo-ry to God in the high-est; glo-ry to God, glo-ry to God, and peace to God's peo-ple on earth.

For you a-lone are the Ho-ly One, you a-lone are the Lord, you a-lone are the Most High, Je-sus Christ, with the Ho-ly Spir-it, in the glo-ry of God the Fa-ther. A - men.

C Glo-ry to God, glo-ry to God, glo-ry to God in the high-est; glo-ry to God, glo-ry to God, and peace to God's peo-ple on earth, and peace to God's peo-ple on earth.

PRAYER OF THE DAY

The salutation may precede the prayer.

P The Lord be with you.

C **And also with you.**

P Let us pray. *(The Prayer of the Day is said, concluding:)*

C **Amen**

WORD

Sit

FIRST READING

 A reading from _____.

After the reading, the reader may say: The word of the Lord.
All may respond: **Thanks be to God.**

PSALM

The Psalm is sung or said.

SECOND READING

 A reading from _____.

After the reading, the reader may say: The word of the Lord.
All may respond: **Thanks be to God.**

Stand

GOSPEL ACCLAMATION

The appointed verse may be sung by the choir, or the congregation may sing a general acclamation or a hymn.

GENERAL

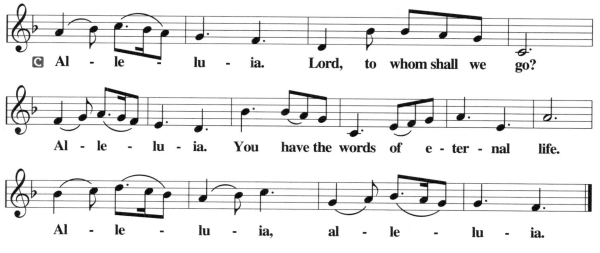

Al - le - lu - ia. Lord, to whom shall we go?

Al - le - lu - ia. You have the words of e - ter - nal life.

Al - le - lu - ia, al - le - lu - ia.

LENT

Re - turn to the Lord, your God, re - turn

to the Lord, your God, who is grac - ious

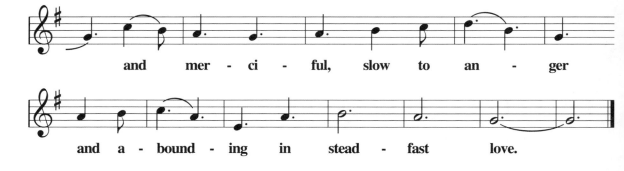

and mer - ci - ful, slow to an - ger

and a - bound - ing in stead - fast love.

GOSPEL

The Gospel is announced.

℗ The Holy Gospel according to _____, the _____ chapter.

℃ Glory to you, O Lord.

After the reading:

℗ The Gospel of the Lord.

℃ Praise to you, O Christ.

Sit

SERMON

Silence for reflection may follow.

Stand

HYMN OF THE DAY

CREED

A Creed may be said: the Nicene Creed, on all festivals and on Sundays in the seasons of Advent/Christmas and Lent/Easter; the Apostles' Creed, at other times. When Holy Baptism or another rite with a creed is celebrated, this creed may be omitted.

NICENE CREED

℃ We believe in one God,
the Father, the Almighty,
maker of heaven and earth,
of all that is, seen and unseen.

We believe in one Lord, Jesus Christ,
the only Son of God,
eternally begotten of the Father,
God from God, Light from Light,
true God from true God,
begotten, not made,
of one Being with the Father.
Through him all things were made.

For us and for our salvation
    he came down from heaven;
    by the power of the Holy Spirit
        he became incarnate from the virgin Mary, and was made man.
For our sake he was crucified under Pontius Pilate;
    he suffered death and was buried.
    On the third day he rose again
        in accordance with the Scriptures;
    he ascended into heaven
        and is seated at the right hand of the Father.
He will come again in glory to judge the living and the dead,
    and his kingdom will have no end.

We believe in the Holy Spirit, the Lord, the giver of life,
    who proceeds from the Father and the Son.
    With the Father and the Son he is worshiped and glorified.
    He has spoken through the prophets.
    We believe in one holy catholic and apostolic Church.
    We acknowledge one Baptism for the forgiveness of sins.
    We look for the resurrection of the dead,
        and the life of the world to come. Amen

APOSTLES' CREED

C I believe in God, the Father almighty,
    creator of heaven and earth.

I believe in Jesus Christ, his only Son, our Lord.
    He was conceived by the power of the Holy Spirit
        and born of the virgin Mary.
    He suffered under Pontius Pilate,
        was crucified, died, and was buried.
    He descended into hell.*
    On the third day he rose again.
    He ascended into heaven,
        and is seated at the right hand of the Father.
    He will come again to judge the living and the dead.

I believe in the Holy Spirit,
    the holy catholic Church,
    the communion of saints,
    the forgiveness of sins,
    the resurrection of the body,
    and the life everlasting. Amen

*Or, He descended to the dead.

THE PRAYERS

The Prayers begin with these or similar words:

Ⓐ Let us pray for the whole people of God in Christ Jesus,
and for all people according to their needs.

Prayers are included for the whole Church, the nations, those in need, the parish, and special concerns. The congregation may be invited to offer other petitions. The minister gives thanks for the faithful departed, especially for those who recently have died.

Each portion of the prayers concludes with these or similar words:

	OR
Ⓐ Lord, in your mercy,	Ⓐ Hear us, O God;
Ⓒ **hear our prayer.**	Ⓒ **your mercy is great.**

The prayers conclude with these or similar words:

Ⓟ Into your hands, O Lord, we commend all for whom we pray,
trusting in your mercy; through your Son, Jesus Christ our Lord.
Ⓒ **Amen**

MEAL

Stand

PEACE

The Peace is shared.

Ⓟ The peace of the Lord be with you always.
Ⓒ **And also with you.**

The ministers and congregation may greet one another with a gesture of peace, using these or similar words: **Peace be with you.**

Sit

PRESENTATION OF THE GIFTS

The Offering is received as the Lord's Table is prepared.

The appointed Offertory may be sung by the choir as the gifts are presented, or the congregation may sing the following offertory, or an appropriate hymn or psalm may be sung.

Let the vine-yards be fruit - ful, Lord, and fill to the brim our cup of

bless - ing. Gath - er a har - vest from the seeds that were sown,

that we may be fed with the bread of life.

Gath-er the hopes and dreams of all; u - nite them with the prayers we

of - fer now. Grace our ta - ble with your pres - ence, Lord,

and give us a fore - taste of the feast to come.

After the gifts have been presented, one of these prayers or another offertory prayer is said.

Ⓐ Let us pray.

Ⓐ Blessed are you,
**Ⓒ O Lord our God,
maker of all things.
Through your goodness
you have blessed us with these gifts.
With them we offer ourselves
to your service
and dedicate our lives
to the care and redemption
of all that you have made,
for the sake of him
who gave himself for us,
Jesus Christ our Lord. Amen** (240)

OR

Ⓐ Let us pray.

Ⓐ Merciful God,
**Ⓒ we offer with joy and thanksgiving
what you have first given us —
our selves,
our time,
and our possessions,
signs of your gracious love.
Receive them
for the sake of him
who offered himself for us,
Jesus Christ our Lord. Amen** (239)

GREAT THANKSGIVING

The Great Thanksgiving is begun by the presiding minister.

Ⓟ The Lord be with you.
Ⓒ **And also with you.**

Ⓟ Lift up your hearts.
Ⓒ **We lift them to the Lord.**

Ⓟ Let us give thanks to the Lord our God.
Ⓒ **It is right to give our thanks and praise.**

Here the minister continues with the proper preface.

ADVENT

Ⓟ It is indeed right and salutary that we should at all times
    and in all places offer thanks and praise to you,
    O Lord, holy Father, almighty and everliving God.
You comforted your people with the promise of the Redeemer,
    through whom you will also make all things new
    in the day when he comes again to judge the world in righteousness.
And so, with the Church on earth and the hosts of heaven,
    we praise your name and join their unending hymn:

CHRISTMAS

Ⓟ It is indeed right and salutary that we should at all times
    and in all places offer thanks and praise to you,
    O Lord, holy Father, through Christ our Lord.
In the wonder and mystery of the Word made flesh
    you have opened the eyes of faith
    to a new and radiant vision of your glory;
    that, beholding the God made visible,
    we may be drawn to love the God whom we cannot see.
And so, with the Church on earth and the hosts of heaven,
    we praise your name and join their unending hymn:

EPIPHANY

Ⓟ It is indeed right and salutary that we should at all times
    and in all places offer thanks and praise to you,
    O Lord, holy Father, through Christ our Lord.
Sharing our life, he lived among us
    to reveal your glory and love,
    that our darkness should give way to his own brilliant light.
And so, with the Church on earth and the hosts of heaven,
    we praise your name and join their unending hymn:

LENT

Ⓟ It is indeed right and salutary that we should at all times
    and in all places offer thanks and praise to you,
    O Lord, holy Father, through Christ our Lord.

You bid your people cleanse their hearts
  and prepare with joy for the paschal feast.
Renew our zeal in faith and life,
  and bring us to the fullness of grace that belongs to the children of God.
And so, with the Church on earth and the hosts of heaven,
  we praise your name and join their unending hymn:

PASSION (I)

ℙ It is indeed right and salutary that we should at all times
  and in all places offer thanks and praise to you,
    O Lord, holy Father, through Christ our Lord;
who on the tree of the cross gave salvation to all,
  that, where death began, there life might be restored,
  and that he, who by a tree once overcame,
    might by a tree be overcome.
And so, with the Church on earth and the hosts of heaven,
  we praise your name and join their unending hymn:

PASSION (II)

ℙ It is indeed right and salutary that we should at all times
  and in all places offer thanks and praise to you,
    O Lord, holy Father, through Christ our Lord.
For our sins he was lifted high upon the cross,
  that he might draw the whole world to himself;
  and, by his suffering and death,
  he became the source of eternal salvation
  for all who put their trust in him.
And so, with the Church on earth and the hosts of heaven,
  we praise your name and join their unending hymn:

EASTER

ℙ It is indeed right and salutary that we should at all times
  and in all places offer thanks and praise to you,
    O Lord, holy Father, almighty and everliving God.
But chiefly we are bound to praise you for the glorious resurrection of our Lord;
  for he is the true Passover Lamb who gave himself to take away our sin,
  who by his death has destroyed death,
  and by his rising has brought us to eternal life.
And so, with Mary Magdalene and Peter and all the witnesses of the resurrection,
  with earth and sea and all their creatures,
  and with angels and archangels, cherubim and seraphim,
  we praise your name and join their unending hymn:

ASCENSION

ℙ It is indeed right and salutary that we should at all times
  and in all places offer thanks and praise to you,
    O Lord, holy Father, through Christ our Lord;

who, after his resurrection, appeared openly to his disciples
   and, in their sight, was taken up into heaven,
   that he might make us partakers of his divine nature.
And so, with the Church on earth and the hosts of heaven,
   we praise your name and join their unending hymn:

PENTECOST

℗ It is indeed right and salutary that we should at all times
   and in all places offer thanks and praise to you,
   O Lord, holy Father, through Christ our Lord;
who rose beyond the bounds of death
   and, [on this day,] as he had promised,
   poured out your Spirit of life and power upon the chosen disciples.
At this the whole earth exults in boundless joy.
And so, with the Church on earth and the hosts of heaven,
   we praise your name and join their unending hymn:

HOLY TRINITY

℗ It is indeed right and salutary that we should at all times
   and in all places offer thanks and praise to you,
   O Lord, holy Father, almighty and everliving God.
You have revealed your glory as the glory also of your Son and of the Holy Spirit:
   three persons, equal in majesty, undivided in splendor,
   yet one Lord, one God, ever to be adored in your everlasting glory.
And so, with the Church on earth and the hosts of heaven,
   we praise your name and join their unending hymn:

SUNDAYS AFTER PENTECOST

℗ It is indeed right and salutary that we should at all times
   and in all places offer thanks and praise to you,
   O Lord, holy Father, through Christ our Lord;
who on this day overcame death and the grave,
   and by his glorious resurrection opened to us the way of everlasting life.
And so, with the Church on earth and the hosts of heaven,
   we praise your name and join their unending hymn:

ALL SAINTS

℗ It is indeed right and salutary that we should at all times
   and in all places offer thanks and praise to you,
   O Lord, holy Father, through Christ our Lord.
In the blessedness of your saints
   you have given us a glorious pledge of the hope of our calling;
   that, moved by their witness and supported by their fellowship,
   we may run with perseverance the race that is set before us
   and with them receive the unfading crown of glory.
And so, with the Church on earth and the hosts of heaven,
   we praise your name and join their unending hymn:

CHRIST THE KING

P It is indeed right and salutary that we should at all times
and in all places offer thanks and praise to you,
O Lord, holy Father, through Christ our Lord.
Born as king in David's line,
his power was revealed in weakness,
his majesty in mercy.
Once enthroned upon the cross,
you raised him from death to your right hand,
there to rule forever in your kingdom of justice, love, and peace.
And so, with the Church on earth and the hosts of heaven,
we praise your name and join their unending hymn:

WEEKDAYS

P It is indeed right and salutary that we should at all times
and in all places offer thanks and praise to you,
O Lord, holy Father, through Christ our Lord.
And so, with the Church on earth and the hosts of heaven,
we praise your name and join their unending hymn:

APOSTLES

P It is indeed right and salutary that we should at all times
and in all places offer thanks and praise to you,
O Lord, holy Father, through the great shepherd of your flock, Christ, our Lord;
who after his resurrection sent forth his apostles
to preach the Gospel and teach all nations,
and promised to be with them always, even to the end of the age.
And so, with patriarchs and prophets, with the apostle(s) _____,
and with all the company of heaven,
we praise your name and join their unending hymn:

BAPTISM

P It is indeed right and salutary that we should at all times
and in all places offer thanks and praise to you,
O Lord, holy Father, through Christ our Lord.
In him you have received us as your children, made us citizens of your kingdom,
and given us your Holy Spirit to guide us into all truth.
And so, with the Church on earth and the hosts of heaven,
we praise your name and join their unending hymn:

MARRIAGE

P It is indeed right and salutary that we should at all times
and in all places offer thanks and praise to you,
O Lord, holy Father, almighty and everliving God.
For your love is firm as the ancient earth,
your faithfulness fixed as the heavens.
Creating and enriching and continuing life,
you created us male and female to fulfill one another;

you gave us the gift of marriage which embodies your love
and which, even where your name is not known,
proclaims your love for the whole human family.
And so, with the Church on earth and the hosts of heaven,
we praise your name and join their unending hymn:

BURIAL

℗ It is indeed right and salutary that we should at all times
and in all places offer thanks and praise to you,
O Lord, holy Father, through Christ our Lord;
who brought to light the living hope of a blessed resurrection,
that, in our grief, we may rejoice in full assurance of our change
into the likeness of his glory.
And so, with the Church on earth and the hosts of heaven,
we praise your name and join their unending hymn:

℃ Ho - ly, ho - ly, ho - ly Lord, God of
pow-er and might, heav - en and earth are full of your
glo - ry. Ho - san - na in the high - est.
Bless-ed is he who comes in the name of the Lord.
Ho - san - na in the high - est, Ho -
san - na in the high - est.

The minister continues, using one of the prayers below.

OR

P We give you thanks, Father,
   through Jesus Christ,
   your beloved Son,
   whom you sent in this end of the ages
   to save and redeem us
   and to proclaim to us your will.

He is your Word,
   inseparable from you.
Through him you created all things,
   and in him you take delight.
He is your Word,
   sent from heaven to a virgin's womb.
He there took on our nature
   and our lot
   and was shown forth as your Son,
   born of the Holy Spirit
   and of the virgin Mary.

It is he,
   our Lord Jesus,
   who fulfilled all your will
   and won for you a holy people;
   he stretched out his hands in suffering
   in order to free from suffering
   those who trust you.

It is he
   who, handed over to a death
   he freely accepted,
   in order to destroy death,
   to break the bonds of the evil one,
   to crush hell underfoot,
   to give light to the righteous,
   to establish his covenant,
   and to show forth the resurrection,
   taking bread and
   giving thanks to you, said:
Take and eat;
   this is my body,
   broken for you.
Do this for the remembrance of me.

This prayer continues on page 38.

P Holy, mighty, and merciful Lord,
   heaven and earth are full of your glory.
In great love you sent to us Jesus,
   your Son, who reached out
   to heal the sick and suffering,
   who preached good news to the poor,
   and who, on the cross,
   opened his arms to all.

In the night in which he was betrayed,
   our Lord Jesus took bread,
   and gave thanks; broke it,
   and gave it to his disciples,
   saying: Take and eat;
   this is my body, given for you.
Do this for the remembrance of me.

Again, after supper,
   he took the cup, gave thanks,
   and gave it for all to drink,
   saying: This cup is
   the new covenant in my blood,
   shed for you and for all people
   for the forgiveness of sin.
Do this for the remembrance of me.

Remembering, therefore,
   his death, resurrection, and ascension,
   we await his coming in glory.

Pour out your Holy Spirit,
   that by this Holy Communion
   we may know the unity
   we share with all your people
   in the body of your Son,
   Jesus Christ our Lord.

Through him, with him, in him,
   in the unity of the Holy Spirit,
   all glory and honor is yours,
   almighty Father, now and forever.
C **Amen**

The Lord's Prayer follows on page 39.

In the same way
    he took the cup,
    gave thanks,
    and gave it for all to drink, saying:
This is my blood poured out for you.
Do this for the remembrance of me.

Remembering, then,
    his death and resurrection,
    we lift this bread and cup before you,
    giving you thanks that
    you have made us worthy
    to stand before you
    and to serve you
    as your priestly people.

And we ask you:
    Send your Spirit
    upon these gifts of your Church;
    gather into one all who share this bread and wine;
    fill us with your Holy Spirit
    to establish our faith in truth,
    that we may praise and glorify you
    through your Son Jesus Christ.

Through him
    all glory and honor is yours,
    Almighty Father,
    with the Holy Spirit,
    in your holy Church
    both now and forever.

A - men, a - men, a - men, a - men, a - men.

LORD'S PRAYER

P Let us pray with confidence
in the words our Savior gave us:

C **Our Father in heaven,**
hallowed be your name,
your kingdom come,
your will be done,
on earth as in heaven.
Give us today our daily bread.
Forgive us our sins
as we forgive those
who sin against us.
Save us from the time of trial
and deliver us from evil.
For the kingdom, the power,
and the glory are yours,
now and for ever. Amen

P Lord, remember us in your
kingdom, and teach us to pray:

C **Our Father, who art in heaven,**
hallowed be thy name,
thy kingdom come,
thy will be done,
on earth as it is in heaven.
Give us this day our daily bread;
and forgive us our trespasses,
as we forgive those
who trespass against us;
and lead us not into temptation,
but deliver us from evil.
For thine is the kingdom,
and the power, and the glory,
forever and ever. Amen

Sit

COMMUNION

The communion follows. The bread may be broken for distribution.

As the ministers give the bread and cup to each communicant, they say these words:

The body of Christ, given for you. The blood of Christ, shed for you.
The communicant may say: **Amen**

As the people commune, hymns and other music may be used, and may include the following:

C Lamb of God, you take a-way the sin of the world; have mer-cy on us. Lamb of God, you take a-way the sin of the world; have mer-cy on us. Lamb of God, you take a-way the sin of the world; grant us peace, grant us peace.

After all have returned to their places, the minister may say these or similar words.

P The body and blood of our Lord Jesus Christ strengthen you
and keep you in his grace.

C **Amen**

CANTICLE

A post-communion canticle or an appropriate hymn or song may be sung.

C Thank - ful hearts and voic - es raise; tell ev - 'ry -
one what God has done. Let all who seek the
Lord re - joice and bear Christ's ho - ly name.
Send us with your prom - is - es, O God,
and lead us forth in joy with shouts
of thanks - giv - ing. Al - le - lu - ia.
(Lent) A - men, a - men.

PRAYER

The following or a similar post-communion prayer is said.

Ⓐ Let us pray.

Ⓐ Almighty God, you provide
the true bread from heaven,
your Son, Jesus Christ our Lord.
Grant that we who have received
the Sacrament of his body and blood
may abide in him and he in us,
that we may be filled with
the power of his endless life,
now and forever. (209)
Ⓒ **Amen**

Silence for reflection.

SENDING

BLESSING

The minister blesses the congregation, using this or another appropriate blessing.

Ⓟ Almighty God, Father, ✝ Son, and Holy Spirit,
bless you now and forever.
Ⓒ **Amen**

When there is a procession from the church, a hymn, song, or canticle may be sung.

DISMISSAL

The minister may dismiss the congregation.

Ⓐ Go in peace. Serve the Lord.
Ⓒ **Thanks be to God.**

HOLY COMMUNION
All Times and Places, Setting 6

GATHERING

An order for CONFESSION AND FORGIVENESS (p. 10) may precede this service.

HYMNS, SONGS, AND CANTICLES may be played and sung as the congregation and ministers gather.

With this or a similar biblical GREETING, the minister extends God's welcome.

Ⓟ The grace of our Lord Jesus Christ, the love of God,
and the communion of the Holy Spirit be with you all.
Ⓒ **And also with you.**

When a KYRIE is sung, one of the following or another appropriate litany may be used.

#601   Kyrie (Ghana)
#602   Kyrie (Russia)
#603   Holy God (Trisagion)
#604   Kyrie (Plainsong)
#605   Señor, ten piedad (Caribbean)

When a HYMN OF PRAISE is sung, one of the following or another appropriate hymn, song, or canticle may be used.

#606   Glory to God (*Liturgy of Joy*)
#607   Glory to God (*Mass of Creation*)
#608   This is the Feast of Victory (North America)
#787   Glory to God, We Give You Thanks (Great Britain)
#791   Alabaré (Central America)

The PRAYER OF THE DAY is said, and the congregation responds, **Amen.**

WORD

The Scripture READINGS for the day are proclaimed. Silence for reflection may follow each reading.

The PSALM is sung or said after the first reading.

When a GOSPEL ACCLAMATION is sung, one of the following or another appropriate hymn, song, or canticle may be used.

#609	Hallelujah/Heleluyan	(Native America)
#610	Alleluia	(South Africa)
#611a	Gospel Acclamation: *General*	(Plainsong)
#611b	Gospel Acclamation: *Lent*	(Plainsong)
#612	Halle, Halle, Hallelujah	(Caribbean)
#613	Celtic Alleluia	(North America)
#614	Praise to You, O Christ, Our Savior	(Lent)
#615	Return to the Lord	(Lent)

The GOSPEL is proclaimed.

The minister announces the Gospel:

Ⓟ The Holy Gospel according to _____, the _____ chapter.
Ⓒ **Glory to you, O Lord.**

After the reading:

Ⓟ The Gospel of the Lord.
Ⓒ **Praise to you, O Christ.**

The SERMON follows. Silence for reflection may follow the sermon.

The HYMN OF THE DAY, a song, or canticle is sung.

A CREED may be said: the Nicene Creed (p. 32 or 54), on all festivals and on Sundays in the seasons of Advent/Christmas and Lent/Easter; the Apostles' Creed (p. 33 or 55), at other times.

THE PRAYERS for the Church, the nations, those in need, the parish, and special concerns are offered, including thanks for the faithful departed.

Each portion of the prayers concludes with these or similar words:

OR

Ⓐ Lord, in your mercy,
Ⓒ **hear our prayer.**

Ⓐ Hear us, O God;
Ⓒ **your mercy is great.**

The minister concludes the prayers, and the congregation responds, **Amen.**

MEAL

The PEACE is shared.

P The peace of the Lord be with you always.

C **And also with you.**

The ministers and congregation may greet one another with a gesture of peace, using these or similar words: **Peace be with you.**

The OFFERING is received as the Lord's Table is prepared.

During the PRESENTATION OF THE GIFTS, one of the following or another appropriate hymn, song, or canticle may be sung.

#705   As the Grains of Wheat
#732   Create in Me a Clean Heart
#758   Come to Us, Creative Spirit
#759   Accept, O Lord, the Gifts We Bring
#760   For the Fruit of All Creation
#761   Now We Offer

This or a similar offertory prayer may be said after the gifts have been presented.

A Let us pray.

A Blessed are you,

C **O Lord, our God, maker of all things.**
Through your goodness you have blessed us with these gifts.
With them we offer ourselves to your service and dedicate our lives
to the care and redemption of all that you have made,
for the sake of him who gave himself for us, Jesus Christ our Lord. Amen (240)

The GREAT THANKSGIVING is begun by the presiding minister.

P The Lord be with you.

C **And also with you.**

P Lift up your hearts.

C **We lift them to the Lord.**

P Let us give thanks to the Lord our God.

C **It is right to give our thanks and praise.**

The Great Thanksgiving continues, using one of the eucharistic prayers provided in the leaders edition. The congregation responds to a seasonal preface with "Holy, holy, holy Lord," using one of the following or another appropriate setting.

#616   Holy, holy, holy Lord (*Land of Rest*)
#617   Holy, holy, holy Lord (*Deutsche Messe*)
#618   Holy, holy, holy Lord (North America)
#619   Holy, holy, holy Lord (*Mass of Creation*)

The minister continues the prayer of thanksgiving, remembering God's mighty deeds of salvation in creation and especially in the person of Jesus Christ. After remembering Jesus' word of promise and his command to celebrate this meal, the congregation may say or sing this acclamation of faith:

P̄ …we proclaim the Lord's death until he comes.

C̄ Christ has died. Christ is risen. Christ will come again.

The minister continues the prayer of thanksgiving by remembering the death and resurrection of Jesus and by praying for the presence of the Holy Spirit.

At the conclusion of the prayer, the congregation responds, **Amen.**

All join together in praying the LORD'S PRAYER (p. 39 or 56).

After the bread is broken, the COMMUNION is shared.

When music is used during communion, one of the following or other appropriate hymns, songs, and canticles may be sung.

#620 Agnus Dei (Plainsong)
#621 Lamb of God (North America)
#622 Lamb of God (North America)

While the table is being cleared after the communion, one of the following or another appropriate hymn, song, or CANTICLE may be sung.

#623 Thankful Hearts and Voices Raise (*Liturgy of Joy*)
#624 Now, Lord, You Let Your Servant Go in Peace (*Detroit Folk Mass*)
#625 Now, Lord, You Let Your Servant Go in Peace (North America)
#722 Hallelujah! We Sing Your Praises (South Africa)
#754 Let Us Talents and Tongues Employ (Caribbean)
#801 Thine the Amen, Thine the Praise (North America)

A PRAYER concludes the meal, and the congregation responds, **Amen.**

SENDING

The minister says a BLESSING.

P̄ Almighty God, Father, ✝ Son, and Holy Spirit, bless you now and forever.

C̄ Amen

With a DISMISSAL, the congregation is sent out in mission.

Ā Go in peace. Serve the Lord.

C̄ Thanks be to God.

SERVICE OF WORD AND PRAYER

The leader may announce the day and its significance before the Gathering Song or before the readings.

Stand

GATHERING SONG

GREETING

The leader greets the congregation.

  Ⓛ The grace of our Lord Jesus Christ, the love of God, and the communion of the Holy Spirit be with you all.   2 Corinthians 13:13

  Ⓒ **And also with you.**

Advent to Transfiguration	*Lent to Pentecost*	*Season after Pentecost*
Ⓛ In the beginning was the Word, **Ⓒ and the Word was with God, and the Word was God.** Ⓛ In the Word was life, **Ⓒ and the life was the light of all people.** Ⓛ The Word became flesh and lived among us, **Ⓒ and we have seen his glory, full of grace and truth.**	Ⓛ The word is near you, **Ⓒ on your lips and in your heart.** Ⓛ If you confess with your lips that Jesus is Lord, **Ⓒ and believe in your heart that God raised him from the dead, you will be saved.** Ⓛ Faith comes from what is heard, **Ⓒ and what is heard comes through the word of Christ.**	Ⓛ You are the treasured people of the Lord, **Ⓒ a people holy to the Lord our God.** Ⓛ Keep the words of the Lord in your heart; teach them to your children. **Ⓒ Talk about them when you are at home and when you are away, when you lie down and when you rise.** Ⓛ One does not live by bread alone, **Ⓒ but by every word that comes from the mouth of the Lord.**
John 1	Romans 10	Deuteronomy 26, 11, 8

SCRIPTURE SONG

This canticle or another scripture song or hymn may be sung.

Refrain

C Sal - va - tion be - longs to our God and to Christ the Lamb for - ev - er and ev - er.

I Great and won - der - ful are your deeds, O God of the u - ni - verse; just and true are your ways, O Rul - er of all the na - tions.

Who can fail to hon-or you, Lord, and sing the glo - ry of your name?

II For you a - lone are the Ho - ly One. All na - tions will draw near and wor - ship be - fore you, for your just and ho - ly works have been re - vealed.

Revelation 7:10, 15:3–4

PRAYER OF THE DAY

The salutation may precede the prayer.

L The Lord be with you.
C **And also with you.**

L Let us pray. *(The Prayer of the Day is said, concluding:)*
C **Amen**

WORD

Sit

READINGS

The scriptures appointed for the day are read. Psalms, hymns, songs, or anthems may be sung in response.

Before each reading, the reader may say: A reading from _____.
After each reading, the reader may say: The word of the Lord.
All may respond: **Thanks be to God.**

Stand

GOSPEL ACCLAMATION

This acclamation or a hymn, song, or canticle may be sung before and/or after the Gospel:

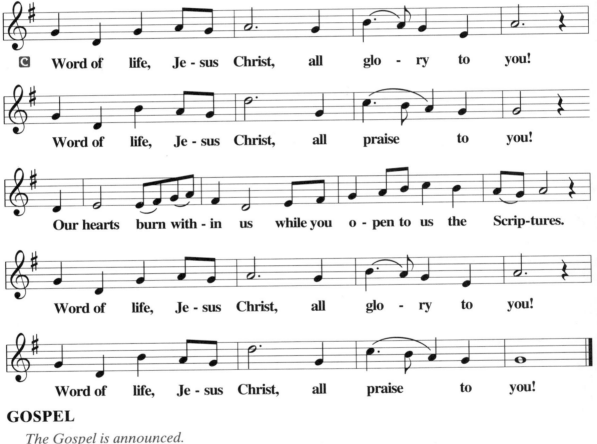

C Word of life, Je-sus Christ, all glo-ry to you!

Word of life, Je-sus Christ, all praise to you!

Our hearts burn with-in us while you o-pen to us the Scrip-tures.

Word of life, Je-sus Christ, all glo-ry to you!

Word of life, Je-sus Christ, all praise to you!

GOSPEL

The Gospel is announced.

L The Holy Gospel according to _____, the _____ chapter.
C **Glory to you, O Lord.**

After the reading:

L The Gospel of the Lord.
C **Praise to you, O Christ.**

Sit

SERMON

Silence for reflection may follow.

RESPONSE TO THE WORD

A song, hymn, or canticle is sung.

As the singing concludes, the leaders may gather near the baptismal font. The response to the Word continues:

Ⓛ In Christ, you have heard the word of truth, the gospel of your salvation.
Ⓒ **We believe in him and are marked with the seal of the promised Holy Spirit.**

Ephesians 1:13–14

Ⓛ Living together in trust and hope, we confess our faith.
Ⓒ **I believe in God, the Father almighty,**
   creator of heaven and earth.

  I believe in Jesus Christ, his only Son, our Lord.
     He was conceived by the power of the Holy Spirit,
        and born of the virgin Mary.
     He suffered under Pontius Pilate,
        was crucified, died, and was buried.
     He descended into hell.[*]
     On the third day he rose again.
     He ascended into heaven,
        and is seated at the right hand of the Father.
     He will come again to judge the living and the dead.

  I believe in the Holy Spirit,
     the holy catholic Church,
     the communion of saints,
     the forgiveness of sins,
     the resurrection of the body,
     and the life everlasting. Amen

  [*]Or, He descended to the dead.

Ⓛ Build yourselves up on your most holy faith;
Ⓒ **pray in the Holy Spirit.**

Jude 20

Ⓛ Keep yourselves in the love of God;
Ⓒ **look forward to the mercy of our Lord Jesus Christ.**

Jude 21

Ⓛ If anyone is in Christ, there is a new creation:
Ⓒ **Everything old has passed away;**
behold, everything has become new!

2 Corinthians 5:17

Ⓛ God has given us the ministry of reconciliation.
Therefore, let us be reconciled to God and to one another.

Kneel/Stand

Silence for reflection and self examination.

Ⓛ Gracious God,

Ⓒ **have mercy on us. In your compassion forgive us our sins,
known and unknown, things done and left undone.
Uphold us by your Spirit so that we may live and serve you in newness of life,
to the honor and glory of your holy name; through Jesus Christ our Lord. Amen**

The leader continues, using the appropriate section below.

OR

Ⓟ Almighty God
have mercy on you,
forgive you all your sins
through our Lord Jesus Christ,
strengthen you in all goodness,
and by the power of the Holy Spirit
keep you in eternal life.

Ⓒ **Amen**

Ⓛ The almighty and merciful Lord
grant us pardon, forgiveness,
and remission of all our sins.

Ⓒ **Amen**

Stand

PEACE

Ⓛ Sisters and brothers, rejoice. Mend your ways, encourage one another,
agree with one another, live in peace.   2 Corinthians 13:11

Ⓛ The peace of the Lord be with you always.

Ⓒ **And also with you.**

*The leaders and congregation may greet one another with a gesture of peace using these or
similar words:* **Peace be with you.**

PRAYER

Sit

OFFERING

An offering is received. Songs, hymns, canticles, and anthems may be played or sung.

Stand

OFFERTORY

*As the gifts are presented, the congregation may sing this Offertory or another appropriate
song, hymn, or canticle.*

Ⓒ *(Advent to Transfiguration)* **Glo - ry   to   you,   God,   for   yours   is   the   earth;**
(Lent to Pentecost) **Glo - ry   to   you,   God,   for   yours   is   the   earth;**
(Season after Pentecost) **Glo - ry   to   you,   God,   for   yours   is   the   earth;**

yours is the prom - ise, the bless - ing, the birth.
yours the ho - san - nas, the dy - ing, re - birth.
yours the a - noint - ing, the ra - di - ant worth.

Ours the re - joic - ing for Word giv - en frame;
Ours the re - joic - ing for na - ture re - claimed;
Ours the re - joic - ing for spir - its a - flame;

ours the thanks - giv - ing to your ho - ly name.

Ours be the tell - ing of deeds great - ly done;

yours be the glo - ry, O God, yours a - lone.

At the conclusion of the Offertory, one of these prayers or another offertory prayer may be said.

Advent to Transfiguration	*Lent to Pentecost*	*Season after Pentecost*

Ⓛ Let us pray.

Ⓛ Merciful God,
**Ⓒ in the mystery of
the Word made flesh,
you embrace our lives
with your great love
for humanity. With joy
and gladness we ask that
these gifts may be for
many a sign of that love,
and that we may continue
to share in your divine
life, through Jesus Christ
our Lord. Amen** (575)

Ⓛ Let us pray.

Ⓛ Gracious God,
**Ⓒ in the abundance of
your steadfast love, you
call us from death to life,
from silence to speech,
from idleness to action.
With these gifts we
offer ourselves to you,
and with the Church
through all the ages
we give thanks for your
saving love in Jesus Christ
our Lord. Amen** (576)

Ⓛ Let us pray.

Ⓛ God, our Creator,
**Ⓒ you open wide
your hand and
satisfy the desire of
every living creature.
With these gifts
we bless you for your
tender nurture and care.
Help us to delight
in your will and
walk in your ways,
through Jesus Christ
our Lord. Amen** (577)

THE PRAYERS

The prayers begin with these or similar words:

Ⓛ As God's people called to love one another,
let us pray for the needs of the Church, the human family, and all the world.

Prayers are included for the whole Church, the nations, those in need, the parish, and special concerns. The congregation may be invited to offer other petitions. The leader gives thanks for the faithful departed, especially for those who recently have died.

Each portion of the prayers concludes with these or similar words:

OR

Ⓛ Hear us, O God;
Ⓒ **your mercy is great.**

Ⓛ God of mercy,
Ⓒ **hear our prayer.**

The prayers conclude with these or similar words:

Ⓛ All these things and whatever else you see that we need, grant us, O God,
for the sake of Christ who died and rose again, and now lives and reigns with you
and the Holy Spirit, one God, forever and ever.
Ⓒ **Amen**

LORD'S PRAYER

Ⓛ Let us pray with confidence
in the words our Savior gave us:

Ⓒ **Our Father in heaven,**
hallowed be your name,
your kingdom come,
your will be done,
on earth as in heaven.
Give us today our daily bread.
Forgive us our sins
as we forgive those
who sin against us.
Save us from the time of trial
and deliver us from evil.
For the kingdom, the power,
and the glory are yours,
now and forever. Amen

Ⓛ Lord, remember us in your
kingdom, and teach us to pray:

Ⓒ **Our Father, who art in heaven,**
hallowed be thy name,
thy kingdom come,
thy will be done,
on earth as it is in heaven.
Give us this day our daily bread;
and forgive us our trespasses,
as we forgive those
who trespass against us;
and lead us not into temptation,
but deliver us from evil.
For thine is the kingdom,
and the power, and the glory,
forever and ever. Amen

BLESSING

The blessing of God is announced, using one of these or other appropriate words.

OR

P Almighty God,
Father, ☩ Son, and Holy Spirit,
bless you now and forever.
C **Amen**

L May the God and Father of
our Lord Jesus Christ fill you
with every spiritual blessing.
C **Amen**

L May the God of faithfulness and
encouragement grant you to live
in harmony with one another,
in accordance with Christ Jesus.
C **Amen**

L May the God of hope fill you
with all joy and peace in believing,
so that you may abound in hope
by the power of the Holy Spirit.
C **Amen**   Romans 15

SENDING SONG

A hymn, song, or canticle may be sung as the people are sent forth.

DISMISSAL

The leader may dismiss the congregation.

L Go in peace. Serve the Lord.
C **Thanks be to God.**

PRAYING TOGETHER
Ecumenical Texts
English Language Liturgical Consultation (1988)

KYRIE

Lord, have mercy.   Christ, have mercy.   Lord, have mercy.

GLORY TO GOD

Glory to God in the highest,
and peace to God's people on earth.

Lord God, heavenly King,
almighty God and Father,
    we worship you, we give you thanks,
    we praise you for your glory.

Lord Jesus Christ, only Son of the Father,
Lord God, Lamb of God,
you take away the sin of the world:
    have mercy on us;
you are seated at the right hand of the Father:
    receive our prayer.

For you alone are the Holy One,
you alone are the Lord,
you alone are the Most High,
    Jesus Christ,
    with the Holy Spirit,
    in the glory of God the Father. Amen

NICENE CREED

We believe in one God,
    the Father, the Almighty,
    maker of heaven and earth,
    of all that is, seen and unseen.

We believe in one Lord, Jesus Christ,
    the only Son of God,
    eternally begotten of the Father,
    God from God, Light from Light,

true God from true God,
begotten, not made,
of one Being with the Father;
through him all things were made.
For us and for our salvation
    he came down from heaven,
    was incarnate of the Holy Spirit and the Virgin Mary
    and became truly human.
    For our sake he was crucified under Pontius Pilate;
    he suffered death and was buried.
    On the third day he rose again
    in accordance with the Scriptures;
    he ascended into heaven
    and is seated at the right hand of the Father.
    He will come again in glory to judge the living and the dead,
    and his kingdom will have no end.

We believe in the Holy Spirit, the Lord, the giver of life,
    who proceeds from the Father and the Son,
    who with the Father and the Son is worshiped and glorified,
    who has spoken through the prophets.
    We believe in one holy catholic and apostolic Church.
    We acknowledge one baptism for the forgiveness of sins.
    We look for the resurrection of the dead,
    and the life of the world to come. Amen

APOSTLES' CREED

I believe in God, the Father almighty,
    creator of heaven and earth.

I believe in Jesus Christ, God's only Son, our Lord,
    who was conceived by the Holy Spirit,
    born of the Virgin Mary,
    suffered under Pontius Pilate,
    was crucified, died, and was buried;
    he descended to the dead.
    On the third day he rose again;
    he ascended into heaven,
    he is seated at the right hand of the Father,
    and he will come to judge the living and the dead.

I believe in the Holy Spirit,
    the holy catholic Church,
    the communion of saints,
    the forgiveness of sins,
    the resurrection of the body,
    and the life everlasting. Amen

THANKSGIVING

The Lord be with you.
  And also with you.
Lift up your hearts.
  We lift them to the Lord.
Let us give thanks to the Lord our God.
  It is right to give our thanks and praise.

Holy, holy, holy Lord, God of power and might,
heaven and earth are full of your glory.
  Hosanna in the highest.
Blessed is he who comes in the name of the Lord.
  Hosanna in the highest.

OUR FATHER

Our Father in heaven,
  hallowed be your name,
  your kingdom come,
  your will be done,
    on earth as in heaven.
Give us today our daily bread.
Forgive us our sins
  as we forgive those who sin against us.
Save us from the time of trial
  and deliver us from evil.
For the kingdom, the power, and the glory are yours
  now and for ever. Amen

LAMB OF GOD

Lamb of God, you take away the sin of the world, have mercy on us.
Lamb of God, you take away the sin of the world, have mercy on us.
Lamb of God, you take away the sin of the world, grant us peace.

CANTICLE

Now, Lord, you let your servant go in peace:
  your word has been fulfilled.
My own eyes have seen the salvation
  which you have prepared in the sight of every people:
a light to reveal you to the nations
  and the glory of your people Israel.

EUCHARISTIC PRAYERS

EUCHARISTIC PRAYER I

Ⓟ Holy God, mighty Lord, gracious Father:
Endless is your mercy and eternal your reign.
You have filled all creation with light and life;
   heaven and earth are full of your glory.

Through Abraham
   you promised to bless all nations.
You rescued Israel, your chosen people.
Through the prophets you renewed your promise;
   and, at this end of all the ages,
   you sent your Son,
   who in words and deeds proclaimed your kingdom
   and was obedient to your will, even to giving his life.

In the night in which he was betrayed,
   our Lord Jesus took bread,
   and gave thanks; broke it,
   and gave it to his disciples,
   saying: Take and eat;
   this is my body, given for you.
Do this for the remembrance of me.

Again, after supper,
   he took the cup, gave thanks,
   and gave it for all to drink,
   saying: This cup is
   the new covenant in my blood,
   shed for you and for all people
   for the forgiveness of sin.
Do this for the remembrance of me.

P For as often as we eat of this bread
   and drink from this cup,
   we proclaim the Lord's death until he comes.
C **Christ has died. Christ is risen. Christ will come again.**

P Therefore, gracious Father,
   with this bread and cup
   we remember the life our Lord offered for us.
And, believing the witness of his resurrection,
   we await his coming in power
   to share with us the great and promised feast.
C **Amen. Come, Lord Jesus.**

P Send now, we pray, your Holy Spirit,
   the spirit of our Lord and of his resurrection,
   that we who receive the Lord's body and blood
   may live to the praise of your glory
   and receive our inheritance with all your saints in light.
C **Amen. Come, Holy Spirit.**

P Join our prayers with those of your servants
   of every time and every place,
   and unite them with the ceaseless petitions
   of our great high priest
   until he comes as victorious Lord of all.

Through him, with him, in him,
   in the unity of the Holy Spirit,
   all glory and honor is yours, almighty Father,
   now and forever.
C **Amen**

EUCHARISTIC PRAYER II

P You are indeed holy, O God,
   the fountain of all holiness;
   you bring light from darkness,
   life from death,
   speech from silence.

We worship you for our lives
   and for the world you give us.
We thank you for the new world to come
   and for the love that will rule all in all.

We praise you for the grace
   shown to Israel, your chosen,
   the people of your promise:
   the rescue from Egypt,
   the gift of the promised land,
   the memory of the ancestors,
   the homecoming from exile,
   and the prophets' words that will not be in vain.

In all this we bless you for your only-begotten Son,
   who fulfilled and will fulfill all your promises.

In the night in which he was betrayed,
   our Lord Jesus took bread,
   and gave thanks; broke it,
   and gave it to his disciples,
   saying: Take and eat;
   this is my body, given for you.
Do this for the remembrance of me.

Again, after supper,
   he took the cup, gave thanks,
   and gave it for all to drink,
   saying: This cup is
   the new covenant in my blood,
   shed for you and for all people
   for the forgiveness of sin.
Do this for the remembrance of me.

For as often as we eat of this bread
   and drink from this cup,
   we proclaim the Lord's death until he comes.
Ꮯ Christ has died. Christ is risen. Christ will come again.

Ᵽ Therefore, O God,
   with this bread and cup
   we remember the incarnation of your Son:
   his human birth and the covenant he made with us.
We remember the sacrifice of his life:
   his eating with outcasts and sinners,
   and his acceptance of death.
But chiefly [on this day]
   we remember his rising from the tomb,
   his ascension to the seat of power,
   and his sending of the holy and life-giving Spirit.
   We cry out for the resurrection of our lives,
   when Christ will come again in beauty and power
   to share with us the great and promised feast.
Ꮯ Amen. Come, Lord Jesus.

P Send now, we pray, your Holy Spirit,
   that we and all who share in this bread and cup
   may be united in the fellowship of the Holy Spirit,
   may enter the fullness of the kingdom of heaven,
   and may receive our inheritance
   with all your saints in light.
C **Amen. Come, Holy Spirit.**

P Join our prayers with those of your servants
   of every time and every place,
   and unite them with the ceaseless petitions
   of our great high priest
   until he comes as victorious Lord of all.

Through him, with him, in him,
   in the unity of the Holy Spirit,
   all glory and honor is yours,
   almighty Father,
   now and forever.
C **Amen**

EUCHARISTIC PRAYER III

P You are indeed holy,
   almighty and merciful God;
   you are most holy,
   and great is the majesty of your glory.

You so loved the world that you gave your only Son,
   that whoever believes in him may not perish
   but have eternal life.

Having come into the world,
   he fulfilled for us your holy will
   and accomplished our salvation.

In the night in which he was betrayed,
   our Lord Jesus took bread,
   and gave thanks; broke it,
   and gave it to his disciples,
   saying: Take and eat;
   this is my body, given for you.
Do this for the remembrance of me.

Again, after supper,
    he took the cup, gave thanks,
    and gave it for all to drink,
    saying: This cup is
    the new covenant in my blood,
    shed for you and for all people
    for the forgiveness of sin.
Do this for the remembrance of me.

Remembering, therefore,
    his salutary command,
    his life-giving Passion and death,
    his glorious resurrection and ascension,
    and his promise to come again,
    we give thanks to you,
    Lord God Almighty,
    not as we ought,
    but as we are able;
    and we implore you
    mercifully to accept
    our praise and thanksgiving,
    and, with your Word and Holy Spirit,
    to bless us, your servants,
    and these your own gifts of bread and wine;
    that we and all who share in the body and blood of your Son
    may be filled with heavenly peace and joy,
    and, receiving the forgiveness of sin,
    may be sanctified in soul and body,
    and have our portion with all your saints.

All glory and honor is yours,
    O God, Father, Son, and Holy Spirit,
    in your holy Church,
    now and forever.
C Amen

EUCHARISTIC PRAYER IV

P We give you thanks, Father,
　　through Jesus Christ, your beloved Son,
　　whom you sent in this end of the ages
　　to save and redeem us
　　and to proclaim to us your will.

He is your Word, inseparable from you.
Through him you created all things,
　　and in him you take delight.

He is your Word,
　　sent from heaven to a virgin's womb.
He there took on our nature and our lot
　　and was shown forth as your Son,
　　born of the Holy Spirit and of the virgin Mary.

It is he,
　　our Lord Jesus,
　　who fulfilled all your will
　　and won for you a holy people;
　　he stretched out his hands in suffering
　　in order to free from suffering those who trust you.

It is he
　　who, handed over to a death he freely accepted,
　　in order to destroy death,
　　to break the bonds of the evil one,
　　to crush hell underfoot,
　　to give light to the righteous,
　　to establish his covenant,
　　and to show forth the resurrection,
　　taking bread and giving thanks to you, said:
　　Take and eat; this is my body, broken for you.
Do this for the remembrance of me.

In the same way he took the cup,
　　gave thanks, and gave it for all to drink, saying:
　　This is my blood poured out for you.
Do this for the remembrance of me.

Remembering, then,
　　his death and resurrection,
　　we lift this bread and cup before you,
　　giving you thanks that you have made us worthy
　　to stand before you
　　and to serve you as your priestly people.

And we ask you:
Send your Spirit upon these gifts of your Church;
    gather into one all who share this bread and wine;
    fill us with your Holy Spirit
    to establish our faith in truth,
    that we may praise and glorify you
    through your Son Jesus Christ.

Through him all glory and honor is yours,
    Almighty Father, with the Holy Spirit,
    in your holy Church,
    both now and forever.
C **Amen**

EUCHARISTIC PRAYER V

P Holy God,
    holy and mighty one,
    holy and immortal:
    you we praise and glorify,
    you we worship and adore.

You formed the earth from chaos;
    you encircled the globe with air;
    you created fire for warmth and light;
    you nourish the lands with water.

You molded us in your image,
    and with mercy higher than the mountains,
    with grace deeper than the seas,
    you blessed the Israelites
    and cherished them as your own.

That also we, estranged and dying,
    might be adopted to live in your Spirit,
    you called to us through the life and death of Jesus,
    who in the night in which he was betrayed,
    took bread, and gave thanks;
    broke it, and gave it to his disciples,
    saying: Take and eat;
    this is my body, given for you.
Do this for the remembrance of me.

Again, after supper,
    he took the cup, gave thanks,
    and gave it for all to drink,
    saying: This cup is
    the new covenant in my blood,
    shed for you and for all people
    for the forgiveness of sin.
Do this for the remembrance of me.

Together as the body of Christ,
    we proclaim the Lord's death until he comes:
C **Christ has died. Christ is risen. Christ will come again.**

P With this bread and cup we remember your Son,
    the first-born of your new creation.
We remember his life lived for others,
    and his death and resurrection,
    which renews the face of the earth.
We await his coming
    when, with the world made perfect through your wisdom,
    all our sins and sorrows will be no more.
C **Amen. Come, Lord Jesus.**

P Holy God,
    holy and merciful one,
    holy and compassionate,
    send upon us and this meal
    your Holy Spirit,
    whose breath revives us for life,
    whose fire rouses us to love.
Enfold in your arms all who share this holy food.
Nurture in us the fruits of the Spirit,
    that we may be a living tree,
    sharing your bounty with all the world.
C **Amen. Come, Holy Spirit.**

P Holy and benevolent God,
    receive our praise and petitions,
    as Jesus received the cry of the needy,
    and fill us with your blessing,
    until, needy no longer and bound to you in love,
    we feast forever in the triumph of the Lamb:
    through whom all glory and honor is yours,
    O God, O Living One,
    with the Holy Spirit,
    in your holy Church,
    now and forever.
C **Amen**

EUCHARISTIC PRAYER A
The Season of Advent

P Holy God, the Beginning and the End,
  our Salvation and our Hope,
  we praise you for creating a world of order and beauty.

When we brought on chaos, cruelty and despair,
  you sent the prophets to proclaim your justice and mercy.

At this end of the ages
  your Son Jesus came to bring us your love
  and to heal all the suffering world.

In the night in which he was betrayed,
  our Lord Jesus took bread,
  and gave thanks; broke it,
  and gave it to his disciples,
  saying: Take and eat;
  this is my body, given for you.
Do this for the remembrance of me.

Again, after supper,
  he took the cup, gave thanks,
  and gave it for all to drink,
  saying: This cup is
  the new covenant in my blood,
  shed for you and for all people
  for the forgiveness of sin.
Do this for the remembrance of me.

Remembering, therefore,
  his life, death, and resurrection,
  we await his coming again
  in righteousness and peace.

Send your Spirit on us
  and on this bread and wine we share:
  strengthen our faith,
  increase our hope,
  and bring to birth the justice and joy of your Son.

Through him all glory and honor is yours,
  Almighty Father, with the Holy Spirit,
  in your holy Church,
  both now and forever.
C **Amen**

EUCHARISTIC PRAYER B
The Season of Christmas

Ⓟ Holy God,
   Creator of all and Source of life,
   at the birth of time
   your word brought light into the world.

In the fullness of time,
   you sent your Word, born of Mary,
   to shine in our darkness
   and to make us your daughters and sons.

In the night in which he was betrayed,
   our Lord Jesus took bread,
   and gave thanks; broke it,
   and gave it to his disciples,
   saying: Take and eat;
   this is my body, given for you.
Do this for the remembrance of me.

Again, after supper,
   he took the cup, gave thanks,
   and gave it for all to drink,
   saying: This cup is
   the new covenant in my blood,
   shed for you and for all people
   for the forgiveness of sin.
Do this for the remembrance of me.

Remembering, therefore,
   his birth and life among us,
   his death and resurrection,
   we await his coming again
   when all things will be restored in him.

By your Spirit bless us and this bread and cup,
   that, held and nourished by you,
   we may live as your children,
   shining with the light of your Son.

Through him all glory and honor is yours,
   Almighty Father, with the Holy Spirit,
   in your holy Church,
   both now and forever.
Ⓒ **Amen**

EUCHARISTIC PRAYER C
The Season of Epiphany

Ⓟ Blessed are you, O holy God:
    you are the Life and Light of all.
By your powerful word you created all things.
Through the prophets you called your people to be a light to the nations.

Blessed are you for Jesus, your Son.
He is your Light, shining in our darkness
    and revealing to us your mercy and might.

In the night in which he was betrayed,
    our Lord Jesus took bread,
    and gave thanks; broke it,
    and gave it to his disciples,
    saying: Take and eat;
    this is my body, given for you.
Do this for the remembrance of me.

Again, after supper,
    he took the cup, gave thanks,
    and gave it for all to drink,
    saying: This cup is
    the new covenant in my blood,
    shed for you and for all people
    for the forgiveness of sin.
Do this for the remembrance of me.

Remembering, therefore,
    his preaching and healing,
    his dying and rising,
    and his promise to come again,
    we await that day when all the universe
        will rejoice in your holy and life-giving light.

By your Spirit bless us and this meal,
    that, refreshed with this heavenly food,
    we may be light for the world,
    revealing the brilliance of your Son.

Through him all glory and honor is yours,
    Almighty Father, with the Holy Spirit,
    in your holy Church,
    both now and forever.
Ⓒ **Amen**

EUCHARISTIC PRAYER D
The Season of Lent

P Holy God,
  our living Water and our merciful Guide,
  together with rivers and seas, wells and springs
  we bless and magnify you.

You led your people Israel through the desert,
  and provided them water from the rock.

We praise you for Christ, our Rock and our Water,
  who joined us in our desert,
  pouring out his life for the world.

In the night in which he was betrayed,
  our Lord Jesus took bread,
  and gave thanks; broke it,
  and gave it to his disciples,
  saying: Take and eat;
  this is my body, given for you.
Do this for the remembrance of me.

Again, after supper,
  he took the cup, gave thanks,
  and gave it for all to drink,
  saying: This cup is
  the new covenant in my blood,
  shed for you and for all people
  for the forgiveness of sin.
Do this for the remembrance of me.

Remembering, therefore,
  his life, death, and resurrection,
  we await your salvation for all this thirsty world.

Pour out your Spirit on this holy food
  and on all the baptized gathered for this feast:
  wash away our sin,
  that we may be revived for our journey by the love of Christ.

Through him all glory and honor is yours,
  Almighty Father, with the Holy Spirit,
  in your holy Church,
  both now and forever.
  C **Amen**

EUCHARISTIC PRAYER E
The Season of Easter

P Holy, living, and loving God,
we praise you for creating the heavens and the earth.

We bless you for bringing Noah and his family through the waters of the flood,
for freeing your people Israel from the bonds of slavery,
and for sending your Son to be our Redeemer.

We give you thanks for Jesus
who, living among us,
healed the sick,
fed the hungry,
and with a love stronger than death,
gave his life for others.

In the night in which he was betrayed,
our Lord Jesus took bread,
and gave thanks; broke it,
and gave it to his disciples,
saying: Take and eat;
this is my body, given for you.
Do this for the remembrance of me.

Again, after supper,
he took the cup, gave thanks,
and gave it for all to drink,
saying: This cup is
the new covenant in my blood,
shed for you and for all people
for the forgiveness of sin.
Do this for the remembrance of me.

Remembering, therefore,
his life-giving death and glorious resurrection,
we await your promised life for all this dying world.

Breathe your Spirit on us and on this bread and cup:
carry us in your arms from death to life,
that we may live as your chosen ones,
clothed in the righteousness of Christ.

Through him all honor and glory is yours,
Almighty Father, with the Holy Spirit,
in your holy Church,
both now and forever.
C **Amen**

EUCHARISTIC PRAYER F
The Day of Pentecost

℗ Holy God,
  Breath of life and Fire of love:
  with a mighty wind you brought creation into being,
  and by a pillar of fire you led your people into freedom.

We praise you for the gift of your Son,
  who poured out your Spirit on his disciples of every race and nation.

In the night in which he was betrayed,
  our Lord Jesus took bread,
  and gave thanks; broke it,
  and gave it to his disciples,
  saying: Take and eat;
  this is my body, given for you.
Do this for the remembrance of me.

Again, after supper,
  he took the cup, gave thanks,
  and gave it for all to drink,
  saying: This cup is
  the new covenant in my blood,
  shed for you and for all people
  for the forgiveness of sin.
Do this for the remembrance of me.

Remembering, therefore,
  his death, resurrection,
  and the sending of the holy and life-giving Spirit,
  we await his coming again to renew the face of the earth.

Send now your Holy Spirit upon us and upon this meal:
  anoint us with your gifts of faith, hope, and love,
  that, with thankful hearts,
  we may be witnesses to your Son.

Through him all glory and honor is yours,
  Almighty Father, with the Holy Spirit,
  in your holy Church,
  both now and forever.
  ᏟᏟ **Amen**

EUCHARISTIC PRAYER G
Summer

P Holy God,
    our Maker, Redeemer, and Healer,
    in the harmonious world of your creation
    the plants and animals,
    the seas and stars
    were whole and well in your praise.

When sin had scarred the world,
    you sent your Son to heal our ills
    and to form us again into one.

In the night in which he was betrayed,
    our Lord Jesus took bread,
    and gave thanks; broke it,
    and gave it to his disciples,
    saying: Take and eat;
    this is my body, given for you.
Do this for the remembrance of me.

Again, after supper,
    he took the cup, gave thanks,
    and gave it for all to drink,
    saying: This cup is
    the new covenant in my blood,
    shed for you and for all people
    for the forgiveness of sin.
Do this for the remembrance of me.

Remembering, therefore,
    his acts of healing
    his body given up,
    and his victory over death,
    we await that day when all the peoples of the earth
    will come to the river to enjoy the tree of life.

Send your Spirit upon us and this meal:
    as grains scattered on the hillside become one bread,
    so let your Church be gathered from the ends of the earth,
    that all may be fed with the Bread of life, your Son.

Through him all glory and honor is yours,
    Almighty Father, with the Holy Spirit,
    in your holy Church,
    both now and forever.
C **Amen**

EUCHARISTIC PRAYER H
Autumn

℗ Holy God,
    our Bread of life, our Table, and our Food,
    you created a world in which all might be satisfied by your abundance.

You dined with Abraham and Sarah, promising them life,
    and fed your people Israel with manna from heaven.

You sent your Son to eat with sinners
    and to become food for the world.

In the night in which he was betrayed,
    our Lord Jesus took bread,
    and gave thanks; broke it,
    and gave it to his disciples,
    saying: Take and eat;
    this is my body, given for you.
Do this for the remembrance of me.

Again, after supper,
    he took the cup, gave thanks,
    and gave it for all to drink,
    saying: This cup is
    the new covenant in my blood,
    shed for you and for all people
    for the forgiveness of sin.
Do this for the remembrance of me.

Remembering, therefore,
    his life given for us
    and his rising from the grave,
    we await his coming again to share with us the everlasting feast.

By your Spirit nurture and sustain us with this meal:
    strengthen us to serve all in hunger and want,
    and by this bread and cup make of us the body of your Son.

Through him all glory and honor is yours,
    Almighty Father, with the Holy Spirit,
    in your holy Church,
    both now and forever.
€ **Amen**

EUCHARISTIC PRAYER I
November

Ⓟ Holy God, holy and mighty, holy and immortal:
  surrounded by evil and bordered by death
  we appeal to you,
  our Sovereign, our Wisdom, and our Judge.

We praise you for Christ, who proclaimed your reign of peace
  and promised an end to injustice and harm.

In the night in which he was betrayed,
  our Lord Jesus took bread,
  and gave thanks; broke it,
  and gave it to his disciples,
  saying: Take and eat;
  this is my body, given for you.
Do this for the remembrance of me.

Again, after supper,
  he took the cup, gave thanks,
  and gave it for all to drink,
  saying: This cup is
  the new covenant in my blood,
  shed for you and for all people
  for the forgiveness of sin.
Do this for the remembrance of me.

Remembering, therefore,
  the sacrifice of his life and death
  and the victory of his resurrection,
  we await with all the saints
  his loving redemption of our suffering world.

Send your Spirit on these gifts of bread and wine
  and on all who share in the body and blood of your Son:
  teach us your mercy and justice,
  and make all things new in Christ.

Through him all glory and honor is yours,
  Almighty Father, with the Holy Spirit,
  in your holy Church,
  both now and forever.
Ⓒ **Amen**

PROPERS

ADVENT

FIRST SUNDAY IN ADVENT

Prayer of the Day
Stir up your power, O Lord, and come.
Protect us by your strength and save us
from the threatening dangers of our sins,
for you live and reign with the Father and
the Holy Spirit, one God, now and forever. (1)

A
Isaiah 2:1–5
Psalm 122
*I was glad when they said to me, "Let us go
to the house of the LORD." (Ps. 122:1)*
Romans 13:11–14
Matthew 24:36–44

B
Isaiah 64:1–9
Psalm 80:1–7, 16–18*
*Show the light of your countenance, and we
shall be saved. (Ps. 80:7)*
1 Corinthians 1:3–9
Mark 13:24–37

C
Jeremiah 33:14–16
Psalm 25:1–9**
To you, O LORD, I lift up my soul. (Ps. 25:1)
1 Thessalonians 3:9–13
Luke 21:25–36

Verse
Alleluia. Show us your mercy, O LORD, and
grant us your salvation. Alleluia. (Ps. 85:7)

Offertory
Truly, the LORD's salvation is very near
to those who fear him, that his glory may
dwell in our land. The LORD will indeed
grant prosperity, and our land will yield its
increase. Righteousness shall go before him,
and peace shall be a pathway for his feet.
(Ps. 85:9, 12–13)

Preface: Advent
Color: Blue *or* Purple

* *Psalm 80:1-7, 17-19 (NRSV)*
** *Psalm 25:1–10 (NRSV)*

NOTE: Psalm references in the body of the propers
follow the versification in *Lutheran Book of Worship;*
NRSV equivalents are listed below.

SECOND SUNDAY IN ADVENT

Prayer of the Day
Stir up our hearts, O Lord, to prepare the
way for your only Son. By his coming give
us strength in our conflicts and shed light
on our path through the darkness of this
world; through your Son, Jesus Christ our
Lord, who lives and reigns with you and the
Holy Spirit, one God, now and forever. (2)

A
Isaiah 11:1–10
Psalm 72:1–7, 18–19
In his time the righteous shall flourish. (Ps. 72:7)
Romans 15:4–13
Matthew 3:1–12

B
Isaiah 40:1–11
Psalm 85:1–2, 8–13
*Righteousness and peace shall go before the
LORD. (Ps. 85:13)*
2 Peter 3:8–15a
Mark 1:1–8

C
Malachi 3:1–4 (*or* Baruch 5:1–9)
Luke 1:68–79
*In the tender compassion of our God, the
dawn from on high shall break upon us.
(Luke 1:78)*
Philippians 1:3–11
Luke 3:1–6

Verse
Alleluia. Prepare the way of the Lord,
make his paths straight; all flesh shall see the
salvation of our God. Alleluia. (Luke 3:4, 6)

Offertory
Then people will come from east and west,
from north and south, and will eat in the
kingdom of God. Blessed is the one who
will eat bread in the kingdom of God!
(Luke 13:29; 14:15)

Preface: Advent
Color: Blue *or* Purple

THIRD SUNDAY IN ADVENT

Prayer of the Day
Almighty God, you once called John the Baptist to give witness to the coming of your Son and to prepare his way. Grant us, your people, the wisdom to see your purpose today and the openness to hear your will, that we may witness to Christ's coming and so prepare his way; through Jesus Christ our Lord, who lives and reigns with you and the Holy Spirit, one God, now and forever. (3)

or
Lord, hear our prayers and come to us, bringing light into the darkness of our hearts; for you live and reign with the Father and the Holy Spirit, one God, now and forever. (4)

A
Isaiah 35:1–10
Psalm 146:4–9* or Luke 1:47–55
The LORD lifts up those who are bowed down. (Ps. 146:7) or *My spirit rejoices in God my Savior. (Luke 1:47)*
James 5:7–10
Matthew 11:2–11

B
Isaiah 61:1–4, 8–11
Psalm 126 or Luke 1:47–55
The LORD has done great things for us. (Ps. 126:4) or *The Lord has lifted up the lowly. (Luke 1:52)*
1 Thessalonians 5:16–24
John 1:6–8, 19–28

C
Zephaniah 3:14–20
Isaiah 12:2–6
In your midst is the Holy One of Israel. (Isa. 12:6)
Philippians 4:4–7
Luke 3:7–18

Verse
Alleluia. See, I am sending my messenger ahead of you, who will prepare your way before you. Alleluia. (Matt. 11:10)

Offertory
The LORD says, I will make a covenant of peace with them; it shall be an everlasting covenant with them. My dwelling place shall be with them; and I will be their God, and they shall be my people. (Ezek. 37:26–27)

Preface: Advent
Color: Blue or Purple

*Psalm 146:5–10 (NRSV)

FOURTH SUNDAY IN ADVENT

Prayer of the Day
Stir up your power, O Lord, and come. Take away the hindrance of our sins and make us ready for the celebration of your birth, that we may receive you in joy and serve you always; for you live and reign with the Father and the Holy Spirit, now and forever. (5)

A
Isaiah 7:10–16
Psalm 80:1–7, 16–18*
Show the light of your countenance and we shall be saved. (Ps. 80:7)
Romans 1:1–7
Matthew 1:18–25

B
2 Samuel 7:1–11, 16
Luke 1:47–55 or Psalm 89:1–4, 19–26
The Lord has lifted up the lowly. (Luke 1:52) or *Your love, O LORD, forever will I sing. (Ps. 89:1)*
Romans 16:25–27
Luke 1:26–38

C
Micah 5:2–5a
Luke 1:47–55 or Psalm 80:1–7
The Lord has lifted up the lowly. (Luke 1:52) or *Show the light of your countenance and we shall be saved. (Ps. 80:7)*
Hebrews 10:5–10
Luke 1:39–45 [46–55]

Verse
Alleluia. The virgin shall conceive and bear a son, and they shall name him Emmanuel. Alleluia. (Matt. 1:23)

Offertory
Sing aloud, O daughter Zion; shout, O Israel! Rejoice and exult with all your heart, O daughter Jerusalem! The LORD, your God, is in your midst; he will renew you in his love; he will exult over you with loud singing as on a day of festival. (Zeph. 3:14, 17)

Preface: Advent
Color: Blue or Purple

*Psalm 80:1–7, 17–19 (NRSV)

CHRISTMAS

THE NATIVITY OF OUR LORD
Christmas Eve (I)

Prayer of the Day
Almighty God, you made this holy night shine with the brightness of the true Light. Grant that here on earth we may walk in the light of Jesus' presence and in the last day wake to the brightness of his glory; through your only Son, Jesus Christ our Lord, who lives and reigns with you and the Holy Spirit, one God, now and forever. (6)

A, B, C
Isaiah 9:2–7
Psalm 96
Let the heavens rejoice and the earth be glad.
(Ps. 96:11)
Titus 2:11–14
Luke 2:1–14 [15–20]

Verse
Alleluia. To you is born this day a Savior, who is the Messiah, the Lord. Alleluia. (Luke 2:11)

Offertory
The people who walked in darkness have seen a great light; those who lived in a land of deep darkness—on them light has shined. For a child has been born for us, a son given to us; authority rests upon his shoulders, and he is named Wonderful Counselor, Mighty God, Everlasting Father, Prince of Peace. (Isa. 9:2, 6)

Preface: Christmas
Color: White

THE NATIVITY OF OUR LORD
Christmas Dawn (II)

Prayer of the Day
Almighty God, you have made yourself known in your Son, Jesus, redeemer of the world. We pray that his birth as a human child will set us free from the old slavery of our sin; through Jesus Christ our Lord, who lives and reigns with you and the Holy Spirit, one God, now and forever. (7)

A, B, C
Isaiah 62:6–12
Psalm 97
Light has sprung up for the righteous.
(Ps. 97:11)
Titus 3:4–7
Luke 2:[1–7] 8–20

Verse
Alleluia. The LORD said to me, You are my son; this day have I begotten you. Alleluia.
(Ps. 2:7)

Offertory
The LORD said to me, You are my son; this day have I begotten you. Princely state has been yours from the day of your birth; in the beauty of holiness have I begotten you, like dew from the womb of the morning. (Ps. 2:7; Ps. 110:3)

Preface: Christmas
Color: White

THE NATIVITY OF OUR LORD
Christmas Day (III)

Prayer of the Day
Almighty God, you wonderfully created and yet more wonderfully restored the dignity of human nature. In your mercy, let us share the divine life of Jesus Christ who came to share our humanity, and who now lives and reigns with you and the Holy Spirit, one God, now and forever. (8)

A, B, C
Isaiah 52:7–10
Psalm 98
All the ends of the earth have seen the victory of our God. (Ps. 98:4)
Hebrews 1:1–4 [5–12]
John 1:1–14

Verse
Alleluia. When the fullness of time had come, God sent his Son. Alleluia. (Gal. 4:4)

Offertory

The LORD said to me, You are my son; this day have I begotten you. Ask of me, and I will give you the nations for your inheritance and the ends of the earth for your possession. (Ps. 2:7–8)

Preface: Christmas
Color: White

FIRST SUNDAY AFTER CHRISTMAS

Prayer of the Day

Almighty God, you have made yourself known in your Son, Jesus, redeemer of the world. We pray that his birth as a human child will set us free from the old slavery of our sin; through Jesus Christ our Lord, who lives and reigns with you and the Holy Spirit, one God, now and forever. (7)

or

Almighty God, you wonderfully created and yet more wonderfully restored the dignity of human nature. In your mercy, let us share the divine life of Jesus Christ who came to share our humanity, and who now lives and reigns with you and the Holy Spirit, one God, now and forever. (8)

A

Isaiah 63:7–9
Psalm 148
The splendor of the LORD is over earth and heaven. (Ps. 148:13)
Hebrews 2:10–18
Matthew 2:13–23

B

Isaiah 61:10—62:3
Psalm 148
The splendor of the LORD is over earth and heaven. (Ps. 148:13)
Galatians 4:4–7
Luke 2:22–40

C

1 Samuel 2:18–20, 26
Psalm 148
The splendor of the LORD is over earth and heaven. (Ps. 148:13)
Colossians 3:12–17
Luke 2:41–52

Verse

Alleluia. Let the peace of Christ rule in your hearts. Alleluia. (Col. 3:15)

Offertory

In the beginning was the Word, and the Word was with God, and the Word was God. And the Word became flesh and lived among us, and we have seen his glory, the glory as of the Father's only Son, full of grace and truth. (John 1:1, 14)

Preface: Christmas
Color: White

SECOND SUNDAY AFTER CHRISTMAS

Prayer of the Day

Almighty God, you have filled us with the new light of the Word who became flesh and lived among us. Let the light of our faith shine in all that we do; through your Son, Jesus Christ our Lord, who lives and reigns with you and the Holy Spirit, one God, now and forever. (9)

A, B, C

Jeremiah 31:7–14 (*or* Sirach 24:1–12)
Psalm 147:13–21*
(*or* Wisdom of Solomon 10:15–21)
Worship the LORD, O Jerusalem; praise your God, O Zion. (Ps. 147:13)
Ephesians 1:3–14
John 1:[1–9] 10–18

Verse

Alleluia. All the ends of the earth have seen the victory of our God. Alleluia. (Ps. 98:4)

Offertory

God is light, and in him there is no darkness at all. If we walk in the light as he is in the light, we have fellowship with one another, and the blood of Jesus cleanses us from all sin. (1 John 1:5, 7)

Preface: Christmas
Color: White

Psalm 147:12–20 (NRSV)

EPIPHANY

THE EPIPHANY OF OUR LORD
January 6

Prayer of the Day
Lord God, on this day you revealed your Son to the nations by the leading of a star. Lead us now by faith to know your presence in our lives, and bring us at last to the full vision of your glory, through your Son, Jesus Christ our Lord, who lives and reigns with you and the Holy Spirit, one God, now and forever. (10)

A, B, C
Isaiah 60:1–6
Psalm 72:1–7, 10–14
All kings shall bow down before him.
(Ps. 72:11)
Ephesians 3:1–12
Matthew 2:1–12

Verse
Alleluia. We observed his star in the East, and have come to pay him homage. Alleluia. (Matt. 2:2)

Offertory
Arise, shine; for your light has come, and the glory of the LORD has risen upon you. They shall bring gold and frankincense, and shall proclaim the praise of the LORD. We observed his star in the East, and have come to pay him homage. (Isa. 60:1, 6; Matt. 2:2)

Preface: Epiphany
Color: White

THE BAPTISM OF OUR LORD
First Sunday after the Epiphany

Prayer of the Day
Father in heaven, at the baptism of Jesus in the River Jordan you proclaimed him your beloved Son and anointed him with the Holy Spirit. Make all who are baptized into Christ faithful in their calling to be your children and inheritors with him of everlasting life; through your Son, Jesus Christ our Lord, who lives and reigns with you and the Holy Spirit, one God, now and forever. (11)

A
Isaiah 42:1–9
Psalm 29
The voice of the LORD is upon the waters.
(Ps. 29:3)
Acts 10:34–43
Matthew 3:13–17

B
Genesis 1:1–5
Psalm 29
The voice of the LORD is upon the waters.
(Ps. 29:3)
Acts 19:1–7
Mark 1:4–11

C
Isaiah 43:1–7
Psalm 29
The voice of the LORD is upon the waters.
(Ps. 29:3)
Acts 8:14–17
Luke 3:15–17, 21–22

Verse
Alleluia. You are my Son, the Beloved; with you I am well pleased. Alleluia. (Mark 1:11)

Offertory
Ascribe to the LORD the glory due his name: worship the LORD in the beauty of holiness. The voice of the LORD is upon the waters; the God of glory thunders. The voice of the LORD is a powerful voice; the voice of the LORD is a voice of splendor. (Ps. 29:2–4)

Preface: Epiphany
Color: White

SECOND SUNDAY AFTER THE EPIPHANY

Prayer of the Day

Lord God, you showed your glory and led many to faith by the works of your Son. As he brought gladness and healing to his people, grant us these same gifts and lead us also to perfect faith in him, Jesus Christ our Lord. (12)

A
Isaiah 49:1–7
Psalm 40:1–12*
I love to do your will, O my God. (Ps. 40:9)
1 Corinthians 1:1–9
John 1:29–42

B
1 Samuel 3:1–10 [11–20]
Psalm 139:1–5, 12–17**
You have searched me out and known me. (Ps. 139:1)
1 Corinthians 6:12–20
John 1:43–51

C
Isaiah 62:1–5
Psalm 36:5–10
We feast on the abundance of your house, O Lord. (Ps. 36:8)
1 Corinthians 12:1–11
John 2:1–11

Verse

Alleluia. The LORD said to me: You are my servant in whom I will be glorified. Alleluia. (Isa. 49:3)

Offertory

Jesus revealed his glory, and his disciples believed in him. Everyone serves the good wine first, but you have kept the good wine until now. (John 2:11, 10)

Preface: Epiphany
Color: Green

*Psalm 40:1–11 (NRSV)
**Psalm 139:1–6, 13–18 (NRSV)

THIRD SUNDAY AFTER THE EPIPHANY

Prayer of the Day

Almighty God, you sent your Son to proclaim your kingdom and to teach with authority. Anoint us with the power of your Spirit, that we, too, may bring good news to the afflicted, bind up the brokenhearted, and proclaim liberty to the captive; through your Son, Jesus Christ our Lord. (13)

A
Isaiah 9:1–4
Psalm 27:1, 5–13*
The LORD is my light and my salvation. (Ps. 27:1)
1 Corinthians 1:10–18
Matthew 4:12–23

B
Jonah 3:1–5, 10
Psalm 62:6–14**
In God is my safety and my honor. (Ps. 62:8)
1 Corinthians 7:29–31
Mark 1:14–20

C
Nehemiah 8:1–3, 5–6, 8–10
Psalm 19
The law of the LORD revives the soul. (Ps. 19:7)
1 Corinthians 12:12–31a
Luke 4:14–21

Verse

Alleluia. Jesus went throughout Galilee, teaching, proclaiming the good news, and curing every disease. Alleluia. (Matt. 4:23)

Offertory

I sought the LORD, and he answered me and delivered me out of all my terror. Look upon him and be radiant, and let not your faces be ashamed. I called in my affliction, and the LORD heard me and saved me from all my troubles. (Ps. 34:4–6)

Preface: Epiphany
Color: Green

*Psalm 27:1, 4–9 (NRSV)
**Psalm 62:5–12 (NRSV)

FOURTH SUNDAY
AFTER THE EPIPHANY

Prayer of the Day
O God, you know that we cannot withstand
the dangers which surround us. Strengthen
us in body and spirit so that, with your help,
we may be able to overcome the weakness
that our sin has brought upon us; through
Jesus Christ, your Son our Lord. (14)

A
Micah 6:1–8
Psalm 15
Lord, who may abide upon your holy hill?
(Ps. 15:1)
1 Corinthians 1:18–31
Matthew 5:1–12

B
Deuteronomy 18:15–20
Psalm 111
The fear of the Lord is the beginning of
wisdom. (Ps. 111:10)
1 Corinthians 8:1–13
Mark 1:21–28

C
Jeremiah 1:4–10
Psalm 71:1–6
From my mother's womb you have been my
strength. (Ps. 71:6)
1 Corinthians 13:1–13
Luke 4:21–30

Verse
Alleluia. The Spirit of the Lord is upon me,
because he has anointed me to bring good
news to the poor. Alleluia. (Luke 4:18)

Offertory
Make your face to shine upon your servant;
and in your lovingkindness save me. How
great is your goodness, O Lord, which you
have laid up for those who fear you; which
you have done in the sight of all for those
who put their trust in you. (Ps. 31:16, 19)

Preface: Epiphany
Color: Green

FIFTH SUNDAY
AFTER THE EPIPHANY

Prayer of the Day
Almighty God, you sent your only Son as
the Word of life for our eyes to see and our
ears to hear. Help us to believe with joy
what the Scriptures proclaim, through Jesus
Christ our Lord. (15)

A
Isaiah 58:1–9a [9b–12]
Psalm 112:1–9 [10]
Light shines in the darkness for the upright.
(Ps. 112:4)
1 Corinthians 2:1–12 [13–16]
Matthew 5:13–20

B
Isaiah 40:21–31
Psalm 147:1–12, 21c*
The Lord heals the brokenhearted. (Ps. 147:3)
1 Corinthians 9:16–23
Mark 1:29–39

C
Isaiah 6:1–8 [9–13]
Psalm 138
I will bow down toward your holy temple.
(Ps. 138:2)
1 Corinthians 15:1–11
Luke 5:1–11

Verse
Alleluia. Jesus said: I am the light of the
world. Whoever follows me will never walk
in darkness but will have the light of life.
Alleluia. (John 8:12)

Offertory
Blessed are the poor in spirit, for theirs is
the kingdom of heaven. Blessed are the
meek, for they will inherit the earth. Blessed
are those who hunger and thirst for righteousness, for they will be filled. (Matt. 5:3, 5–6)

Preface: Epiphany
Color: Green

*Psalm 147:1–11, 20c (NRSV)

SIXTH SUNDAY AFTER THE EPIPHANY
Proper 1

Prayer of the Day
Lord God, mercifully receive the prayers of your people. Help us to see and understand the things we ought to do, and give us grace and power to do them; through your Son, Jesus Christ our Lord. (16)

A
Deuteronomy 30:15–20 (or Sirach 15:15–20)
Psalm 119:1–8
Happy are they who walk in the law of the LORD. (Ps. 119:1)
1 Corinthians 3:1–9
Matthew 5:21–37

B
2 Kings 5:1–14
Psalm 30
My God, I cried out to you, and you restored me to health. (Ps. 30:2)
1 Corinthians 9:24–27
Mark 1:40–45

C
Jeremiah 17:5–10
Psalm 1
They are like trees planted by streams of water. (Ps. 1:3)
1 Corinthians 15:12–20
Luke 6:17–26

Verse
Alleluia. Lord, to whom shall we go? You have the words of eternal life. Alleluia. (John 6:68)

Offertory
Behold, God is my helper; it is the LORD who sustains my life. I will offer you a freewill sacrifice and praise your name, O LORD, for it is good. For you have rescued me from every trouble. (Ps. 54:4, 6–7)

Preface: Epiphany
Color: Green

SEVENTH SUNDAY AFTER THE EPIPHANY
Proper 2

Prayer of the Day
God of compassion, keep before us the love you have revealed in your Son, who prayed even for his enemies; in our words and deeds help us to be like him through whom we pray, Jesus Christ our Lord. (18)

or (Year B)
Lord God, we ask you to keep your family, the Church, always faithful to you, that all who lean on the hope of your promises may gain strength from the power of your love; through your Son, Jesus Christ our Lord. (17)

A
Leviticus 19:1–2, 9–18
Psalm 119:33–40
Teach me, O LORD, the way of your statutes. (Ps. 119:33)
1 Corinthians 3:10–11, 16–23
Matthew 5:38–48

B
Isaiah 43:18–25
Psalm 41
Heal me, for I have sinned against you. (Ps. 41:4)
2 Corinthians 1:18–22
Mark 2:1–12

C
Genesis 45:3–11, 15
Psalm 37:1–12, 41–42*
The lowly shall possess the land; they will delight in abundance of peace. (Ps. 37:12)
1 Corinthians 15:35–38, 42–50
Luke 6:27–38

Verse
Alleluia. Sanctify us in the truth; your word is truth. Alleluia. (John 17:17)

Offertory
I appeal to you, therefore, by the mercies of God, to present your bodies as a living sacrifice, holy and acceptable to God, which is your spiritual worship. (Rom. 12:1)

Preface: Epiphany
Color: Green

*Psalm 37:1–11, 39–40 (NRSV)

EIGHTH SUNDAY AFTER THE EPIPHANY
Proper 3

Prayer of the Day
Almighty and everlasting God, ruler of heaven and earth: Hear our prayer and give us your peace now and forever; through your Son, Jesus Christ our Lord. (19)

A
Isaiah 49:8–16a
Psalm 131
Like a child upon its mother's breast, my soul is quieted within me. (Ps. 131:3)
1 Corinthians 4:1–5
Matthew 6:24–34

B
Hosea 2:14–20
Psalm 103:1–13, 22
The LORD is full of compassion and mercy. (Ps. 103:8)
2 Corinthians 3:1–6
Mark 2:13–22

C
Isaiah 55:10–13 (*or* Sirach 27:4–7)
Psalm 92:1–4, 11–14*
The righteous shall flourish like a palm tree. (Ps. 92:11)
1 Corinthians 15:51–58
Luke 6:39–49

Verse
Alleluia. The steadfast love of the LORD never ceases; his mercies never come to an end. Alleluia. (Lam. 3:22)

Offertory
I put my trust in your mercy; my heart is joyful because of your saving help. I will sing to you, O LORD, for you have dealt with me richly. (Ps. 13:5–6)

Preface: Epiphany
Color: Green

*Psalm 92:1–4, 12–15 (NRSV)

THE TRANSFIGURATION OF OUR LORD
Last Sunday after the Epiphany

Prayer of the Day
Almighty God, on the mountain you showed your glory in the transfiguration of your Son. Give us the vision to see beyond the turmoil of our world and to behold the king in all his glory; through your Son, Jesus Christ our Lord, who lives and reigns with you and the Holy Spirit, one God, now and forever. (20)

or

O God, in the transfiguration of your Son you confirmed the mysteries of the faith by the witness of Moses and Elijah, and in the voice from the bright cloud you foreshadowed our adoption as your children. Make us with the king heirs of your glory, and bring us to enjoy its fullness, through Jesus Christ our Lord, who lives and reigns with you and the Holy Spirit, one God, now and forever. (21)

A
Exodus 24:12–18
Psalm 2 *or* Psalm 99
You are my son; this day have I begotten you. (Ps. 2:7) or *Proclaim the greatness of the LORD; worship upon God's holy hill. (Ps. 99:9)*
2 Peter 1:16–21
Matthew 17:1–9

B
2 Kings 2:1–12
Psalm 50:1–6
Out of Zion, perfect in beauty, God shines forth in glory. (Ps. 50:2)
2 Corinthians 4:3–6
Mark 9:2–9

C
Exodus 34:29–35
Psalm 99
Proclaim the greatness of the LORD; worship upon God's holy hill. (Ps. 99:9)
2 Corinthians 3:12—4:2
Luke 9:28–36 [37–43]

Verse
Alleluia. You are the fairest of men; grace flows from your lips. Alleluia. (Ps. 45:2)

Offertory
Beloved, we are God's children now; what we will be has not yet been revealed. What we do know is this: when he is revealed we will be like him, for we will see him as he is. And all who have this hope in him purify themselves, just as he is pure. (1 John 3:2–3)

Preface: Epiphany
Color: White

LENT

ASH WEDNESDAY

Prayer of the Day
Almighty and ever-living God, you hate nothing you have made and you forgive the sins of all who are penitent. Create in us new and honest hearts, so that, truly repenting of our sins, we may obtain from you, the God of all mercy, full pardon and forgiveness; through your Son, Jesus Christ our Lord, who lives and reigns with you and the Holy Spirit, one God, now and forever. (22)

A, B, C
Joel 2:1–2, 12–17 *or* Isaiah 58:1–12
Psalm 51:1–18*
Have mercy on me, O God, according to your lovingkindness. (Ps. 51:1)
2 Corinthians 5:20b—6:10
Matthew 6:1–6, 16–21

Verse
Return to the LORD, your God, who is gracious and merciful, slow to anger, and abounding in steadfast love. (Joel 2:13)

Offertory
Create in me a clean heart, O God, and renew a right spirit within me. Cast me not away from your presence, and take not your Holy Spirit from me. Restore to me the joy of your salvation, and uphold me with your free Spirit. (Ps. 51:10–12)

Preface: Lent
Color: Black *or* Purple

*Psalm 51:1–17 (NRSV)

FIRST SUNDAY IN LENT

Prayer of the Day
Lord God, you led your ancient people through the wilderness and brought them to the promised land. Guide now the people of your Church, that, following our Savior, we may walk through the wilderness of this world toward the glory of the world to come; through your Son, Jesus Christ our Lord, who lives and reigns with you and the Holy Spirit, one God, now and forever. (24)

or

Lord God, our strength, the battle of good and evil rages within and around us, and our ancient foe tempts us with his deceits and empty promises. Keep us steadfast in your Word and, when we fall, raise us again and restore us through your Son, Jesus Christ our Lord, who lives and reigns with you and the Holy Spirit, one God, now and forever. (25)

A
Genesis 2:15–17; 3:1–7
Psalm 32
Mercy embraces those who trust in the LORD. (Ps. 32:11)
Romans 5:12–19
Matthew 4:1–11

B
Genesis 9:8–17
Psalm 25:1–9*
Your paths are love and faithfulness to those who keep your covenant. (Ps. 25:9)
1 Peter 3:18–22
Mark 1:9–15

C
Deuteronomy 26:1–11
Psalm 91:1–2, 9–16
God shall charge the angels to keep you in all your ways. (Ps. 91:11)
Romans 10:8b–13
Luke 4:1–13

Verse
One does not live by bread alone, but by every word that comes from the mouth of God. (Matt. 4:4)

Offertory
Repent and turn from all your transgressions; otherwise iniquity will be your ruin. Cast away from you all the transgressions that you have committed against me, and get yourselves a new heart and a new spirit! For I have no pleasure in the death of anyone, says the Lord GOD. Turn, then, and live. (Ezek. 18:30–32)

Preface: Lent
Color: Purple

*Psalm 25:1–10 (NRSV)

SECOND SUNDAY IN LENT

Prayer of the Day
Eternal God, it is your glory always to have mercy. Bring back all who have erred and strayed from your ways; lead them again to embrace in faith the truth of your Word and to hold it fast; through Jesus Christ your Son our Lord, who lives and reigns with you and the Holy Spirit, one God, now and forever. (26)

A
Genesis 12:1–4a
Psalm 121
It is the LORD who watches over you. (Ps. 121:5)
Romans 4:1–5, 13–17
John 3:1–17

B
Genesis 17:1–7, 15–16
Psalm 22:22–30*
All the ends of the earth shall remember and turn to the LORD. (Ps. 22:26)
Romans 4:13–25
Mark 8:31–38

C
Genesis 15:1–12, 17–18
Psalm 27
In the day of trouble, the LORD shall keep me safe. (Ps. 27:7)
Philippians 3:17—4:1
Luke 13:31–35

Verse
God so loved the world that he gave his only Son, so that everyone who believes in him may not perish but may have eternal life. (John 3:16)

Offertory
What shall I render to the LORD for all his benefits to me? I will offer the sacrifice of thanksgiving and will call on the name of the LORD. I will take the cup of salvation and will call on the name of the LORD.
I will pay my vows to the LORD now in the presence of all his people, in the courts of the LORD's house, in the midst of you, O Jerusalem. (Ps. 116:10–12, 16–17)

Preface: Lent
Color: Purple

*Psalm 22:23–31 (NRSV)

THIRD SUNDAY IN LENT

Prayer of the Day
Eternal Lord, your kingdom has broken into our troubled world through the life, death, and resurrection of your Son. Help us to hear your Word and obey it, so that we become instruments of your redeeming love; through your Son, Jesus Christ our Lord, who lives and reigns with you and the Holy Spirit, one God, now and forever. (28)

or (Year A)
Almighty God, your Son once welcomed an outcast woman because of her faith. Give us faith like hers, that we also may trust only in your love for us and may accept one another as we have been accepted by you; through your Son, Jesus Christ our Lord, who lives and reigns with you and the Holy Spirit, one God, now and forever. (27)

A
Exodus 17:1–7
Psalm 95
Let us shout for joy to the rock of our salvation. (Ps. 95:1)
Romans 5:1–11
John 4:5–42

B
Exodus 20:1–17
Psalm 19
The commandment of the LORD gives light to the eyes. (Ps. 19:8)
1 Corinthians 1:18–25
John 2:13–22

C
Isaiah 55:1–9
Psalm 63:1–8
O God, eagerly I seek you; my soul thirsts for you. (Ps. 63:1)
1 Corinthians 10:1–13
Luke 13:1–9

Verse
Jesus humbled himself and became obedient to the point of death—even death on a cross. (Phil. 2:8)

Offertory
In those days and in that time, says the LORD, the people of Israel and the people of Judah shall come; they shall come weeping as they seek the LORD their God. They shall ask the way to Zion, with faces turned toward it, and they shall come and join themselves to the LORD by an everlasting covenant that will never be forgotten. (Jer. 50:4–5)

Preface: Lent
Color: Purple

FOURTH SUNDAY IN LENT

Prayer of the Day
God of all mercy, by your power to heal and to forgive, graciously cleanse us from all sin and make us strong; through your Son, Jesus Christ our Lord, who lives and reigns with you and the Holy Spirit, one God, now and forever. (29)

A
1 Samuel 16:1–13
Psalm 23
You have anointed my head with oil. (Ps. 23:5)
Ephesians 5:8–14
John 9:1–41

B
Numbers 21:4–9
Psalm 107:1–3, 17–22
The LORD delivered them from their distress. (Ps. 107:19)
Ephesians 2:1–10
John 3:14–21

C
Joshua 5:9–12
Psalm 32
Be glad, you righteous, and rejoice in the LORD. (Ps. 32:12)
2 Corinthians 5:16–21
Luke 15:1–3, 11b–32

Verse
Just as Moses lifted up the serpent in the wilderness, so must the Son of Man be lifted up, that whoever believes in him may have eternal life. (John 3:14–15)

Offertory
Come, let us return to the LORD; for it is he who has torn, and he will heal us; he has struck down, and he will bind us up. After two days he will revive us; on the third day he will raise us up. (Hos. 6:1–2)

Preface: Lent
Color: Purple

FIFTH SUNDAY IN LENT

Prayer of the Day
Almighty God, our redeemer, in our weakness we have failed to be your messengers of forgiveness and hope in the world. Renew us by your Holy Spirit, that we may follow your commands and proclaim your reign of love; through your Son, Jesus Christ our Lord, who lives and reigns with you and the Holy Spirit, one God, now and forever. (30)

A
Ezekiel 37:1–14
Psalm 130
With the LORD there is mercy and plenteous redemption. (Ps. 130:6–7)
Romans 8:6–11
John 11:1–45

B
Jeremiah 31:31–34
Psalm 51:1–13* *or* Psalm 119:9–16
Create in me a clean heart, O God. (Ps. 51:11)
or *I treasure your promise in my heart.
(Ps. 119:11)*
Hebrews 5:5–10
John 12:20–33

C
Isaiah 43:16–21
Psalm 126
Those who sowed with tears will reap with songs of joy. (Ps. 126:6)
Philippians 3:4b–14
John 12:1–8

Verse
The Son of Man came not to be served but to serve, and to give his life a ransom for many. (Mark 10:45)

Offertory
Remember Jesus Christ, raised from the dead, a descendant of David. If we have died with him, we will also live with him; if we endure, we will also reign with him. If we are faithless, he remains faithful— for he cannot deny himself. (2 Tim. 2:8, 11–13)

Preface: Lent
Color: Purple

*Psalm 51:1–12 (NRSV)

HOLY WEEK

SUNDAY OF THE PASSION
PALM SUNDAY

Procession with Palms

A Matthew 21:1–11
B Mark 11:1–11 *or* John 12:12–16
C Luke 19:28–40

Psalm 118:1–2, 19–29
Blessed is he who comes in the name of the
LORD. *(Ps. 118:26)*

Liturgy of the Passion

Prayer of the Day
Almighty God, you sent your Son, our
Savior Jesus Christ, to take our flesh upon
him and to suffer death on the cross. Grant
that we may share in his obedience to your
will and in the glorious victory of his resurrection; through your Son, Jesus Christ our
Lord, who lives and reigns with you and the
Holy Spirit, one God, now and forever. (31)

A
Isaiah 50:4–9a
Psalm 31:9–16
Into your hands, O LORD, *I commend my
spirit. (Ps. 31:5)*
Philippians 2:5–11
Matthew 26:14—27:66 *or* Matthew 27:11–54

B
Isaiah 50:4–9a
Psalm 31:9–16
Into your hands, O LORD, *I commend my
spirit. (Ps. 31:5)*
Philippians 2:5–11
Mark 14:1—15:47 *or* Mark 15:1–39 [40–47]

C
Isaiah 50:4–9a
Psalm 31:9–16
Into your hands, O LORD, *I commend my
spirit. (Ps. 31:5)*
Philippians 2:5–11
Luke 22:14—23:56 *or* Luke 23:1–49

Verse
The hour has come for the Son of Man to
be glorified. (John 12:23)

Offertory
Very truly, I tell you, unless a grain of wheat
falls into the earth and dies, it remains just a
single grain; but if it dies it bears much fruit.
Whoever serves me must follow me, and
where I am, there will my servant be also.
Whoever serves me, the Father will honor.
(John 12:24, 26)

Preface: Passion
Color: Scarlet *or* Purple

MONDAY IN HOLY WEEK

Prayer of the Day
O God, your Son chose the path which led
to pain before joy and the cross before
glory. Plant his cross in our hearts, so that in
its power and love we may come at last to
joy and glory; through your Son, Jesus
Christ our Lord. (34)

A, B, C
Isaiah 42:1–9
Psalm 36:5–11
*Your people take refuge under the shadow of
your wings. (Ps. 36:7)*
Hebrews 9:11–15
John 12:1–11

Verse
May I never boast of anything except the
cross of our Lord Jesus Christ. (Gal. 6:14)

Offertory
I have been crucified with Christ; and it is no
longer I who live, but it is Christ who lives in
me. And the life I now live in the flesh I live
by faith in the Son of God, who loved me
and gave himself for me. (Gal. 2:19–20)

Preface: Passion
Color: Scarlet *or* Purple

TUESDAY IN HOLY WEEK

Prayer of the Day

Lord Jesus, you have called us to follow you. Grant that our love may not grow cold in your service, and that we may not fail or deny you in the hour of trial. (35)

A, B, C

Isaiah 49:1–7
Psalm 71:1–14
From my mother's womb you have been my strength. (Ps. 71:6)
1 Corinthians 1:18–31
John 12:20–36

Verse

May I never boast of anything except the cross of our Lord Jesus Christ. (Gal. 6:14)

Offertory

I have been crucified with Christ; and it is no longer I who live, but it is Christ who lives in me. And the life I now live in the flesh I live by faith in the Son of God, who loved me and gave himself for me. (Gal. 2:19–20)

Preface: Passion
Color: Scarlet *or* Purple

WEDNESDAY IN HOLY WEEK

Prayer of the Day

Almighty God, your Son our Savior suffered at human hands and endured the shame of the cross. Grant that we may walk in the way of his cross and find it the way of life and peace; through your Son, Jesus Christ our Lord. (36)

A, B, C

Isaiah 50:4–9a
Psalm 70
Be pleased, O God, to deliver me. (Ps. 70:1)
Hebrews 12:1–3
John 13:21–32

Verse

May I never boast of anything except the cross of our Lord Jesus Christ. (Gal. 6:14)

Offertory

I have been crucified with Christ; and it is no longer I who live, but it is Christ who lives in me. And the life I now live in the flesh I live by faith in the Son of God, who loved me and gave himself for me. (Gal. 2:19–20)

Preface: Passion
Color: Scarlet *or* Purple

THE THREE DAYS

MAUNDY THURSDAY

Prayer of the Day

Holy God, source of all love, on the night of his betrayal, Jesus gave his disciples a new commandment: To love one another as he had loved them. By your Holy Spirit write this commandment in our hearts; through your Son, Jesus Christ our Lord, who lives and reigns with you and the Holy Spirit, one God, now and forever. (37)

or

Lord God, in a wonderful Sacrament you have left us a memorial of your suffering and death. May this Sacrament of your body and blood so work in us that the way we live will proclaim the redemption you have brought; for you live and reign with the Father and the Holy Spirit, one God, now and forever. (38)

A, B, C

Exodus 12:1–4 [5–10] 11–14
Psalm 116:1, 10–17*
I will take the cup of salvation and call on the name of the LORD. (Ps. 116:11)
1 Corinthians 11:23–26
John 13:1–17, 31b–35

Verse

As often as you eat this bread and drink the cup, you proclaim the Lord's death until he comes. (1 Cor. 11:26)

Offertory

The LORD, the LORD, a God merciful and gracious, slow to anger, and abounding in steadfast love and faithfulness, keeping steadfast love for the thousandth generation, forgiving iniquity and transgression and sin. (Exod. 34:6–7)

Preface: Passion
Color: Scarlet *or* White

*Psalm 116:1–2, 12–19 (NRSV)

GOOD FRIDAY

Prayer of the Day

Almighty God, we ask you to look with
mercy on your family, for whom our Lord
Jesus Christ was willing to be betrayed and
to be given over to the hands of sinners and
to suffer death on the cross; who now lives
and reigns with you and the Holy Spirit, one
God, forever and ever. (39)

or

Lord Jesus, you carried our sins in your own
body on the tree so that we might have life.
May we and all who remember this day find
new life in you now and in the world to come,
where you live and reign with the Father and
the Holy Spirit, now and forever. (40)

A, B, C

Isaiah 52:13—53:12
Psalm 22
*My God, my God, why have you forsaken
me? (Ps. 22:1)*
Hebrews 10:16–25
or Hebrews 4:14–16; 5:7–9
John 18:1—19:42

THE RESURRECTION
OF OUR LORD
Vigil of Easter

Prayer of the Day

O God, who made this most holy night to
shine with the glory of the Lord's resurrection: Stir up in your Church that Spirit of
adoption which is given to us in Baptism,
that we, being renewed both in body and
mind, may worship you in sincerity and
truth; through Jesus Christ our Lord, who
lives and reigns with you, in the unity of the
Holy Spirit, one God, now and forever. (573)

Creation

First Reading: Genesis 1:1—2:4a
Response: Psalm 136:1–9, 23–36
God's mercy endures forever. (Ps. 136:1b)

Almighty God, you wonderfully created the
dignity of human nature and yet more
wonderfully restored it. In your mercy, let
us share the divine life of him who came to
share our humanity, Jesus Christ your Son,
our Lord. (51)

The Flood

Second Reading: Genesis 7:1–5, 11–18,
8:6–18, 9:8–13
Response: Psalm 46
*The LORD of hosts is with us; the God of
Jacob is our stronghold. (Ps. 46:4)*

Almighty God, you have placed the rain-
bow in the skies as a sign of your covenant
with all living things. Grant that we, who are
saved through water and the Spirit, may
worthily offer to you our sacrifice of
thanksgiving; through Jesus Christ our
Lord. (578)

The Testing of Abraham

Third Reading: Genesis 22:1–18
Response: Psalm 16
You will show me the path of life. (Ps. 16:11)

God of all the faithful, you promised
Abraham that he would become the father
of all nations, and through this paschal
mystery you increase your chosen people
throughout the world. Help us to respond
to your call by joyfully accepting the new
life of grace; through your Son, Jesus Christ
our Lord. (53)

Israel's Deliverance at the Red Sea

Fourth Reading: Exodus 14:10–31; 15:20–21
Response: Exodus 15:1b–13, 17–18
*I will sing to the LORD who has triumphed
gloriously. (Exod. 15:1)*

O God, whose wonderful deeds of old shine
forth even to our day: By the power of your
mighty arm you once delivered your people
from slavery under Pharaoh, a sign for us of
the salvation of all nations by the water of
Baptism. Grant that all peoples of the earth
may be numbered among the offspring of
Abraham and may rejoice in the inheritance of Israel; through your Son, Jesus
Christ our Lord. (54)

Salvation Freely Offered to All

Fifth Reading: Isaiah 55:1–11
Response: Isaiah 12:2–6
*With joy you will draw water from the wells
of salvation. (Isa. 12:3)*

O God, you have created all things by the
power of your Word, and you renew the
earth by your Spirit. Give now the water of
life to those who thirst for you, that they
may bring forth abundant fruit in your
glorious kingdom; through your Son, Jesus
Christ our Lord. (55)

The Wisdom of God

Sixth Reading: Proverbs 8:1–8, 19–21; 9:4b–6 *or* Baruch 3:9–15, 32—4:4
Response: Psalm 19
The statutes of the LORD are just and rejoice the heart. (Ps. 19:8)

O God, you increase your Church by continuing to call all peoples to salvation. Let the cleansing waters of Baptism flow, and by your love watch over those whom you have called; through your Son, Jesus Christ our Lord. (56)

A New Heart and a New Spirit

Seventh Reading: Ezekiel 36:24–28
Response: Psalm 42 and Psalm 43
My soul is athirst for the living God. (Ps. 42:2)

Almighty and everlasting God, in the mystery of the dying and rising of Christ you established a new covenant of reconciliation. Cleanse our hearts and give a new spirit to your people, that all those reborn in Baptism may show forth in their lives what they profess by their faith; through your Son, Jesus Christ our Lord. (579)

The Valley of the Dry Bones

Eighth Reading: Ezekiel 37:1–14
Response: Psalm 143
Revive me, O LORD, for your name's sake. (Ps. 143:11)

O God, by the Passover of the Son you have brought us out of sin into righteousness and out of death into life. Give us such an understanding of your mercy that, in receiving the gifts of Word and Sacrament now, we may learn to hope for all your gifts to come; through your Son, Jesus Christ our Lord. (57)

The Gathering of God's People

Ninth Reading: Zephaniah 3:14–20
Response: Psalm 98
Lift up your voice, rejoice and sing. (Ps. 98:5)

O God, strength of the powerless and light in all darkness: look in mercy upon your Church, that wonderful and sacred mystery. Bring to completion your work of salvation; let the whole world experience and see that what was fallen is being raised up, that what was old is being made new, and that all things are being restored to wholeness through him from whom they first took being, your Son, Jesus Christ our Lord. (580)

The Call of Jonah

Tenth Reading: Jonah 3:1-10
Response: Jonah 2:1-3 [4-6] 7-9
Deliverance belongs to the LORD. (Jonah 2:9)

O God, you have united all nations in the confession of your name. Now give us the will and the power to do what you command, that the faith of the people whom you call to everlasting life may direct their speech and actions; through your Son, Jesus Christ our Lord. (60)

The Song of Moses

Eleventh Reading: Deuteronomy 31:19-30
Response: Deuteronomy 32:1-4, 7, 36a, 43a
The LORD will give his people justice. (Deut. 32:36)

O God, exaltation of the humble and strength of the righteous: You taught your people through Moses to sing your praise, that the law which he delivered to them might be helpful to us. Show your power among the nations that, in the forgiveness of sins, terror may turn to joy, and fear of retribution to salvation; through your Son, Jesus Christ our Lord. (61)

The Fiery Furnace

Twelfth Reading: Daniel 3:1-29
Response: Song of the Three Young Men 35-65
Sing praise to the LORD and highly exalt him forever. (Song of the Three Young Men 35b)

New Testament Reading: Romans 6:3–11
Response: Psalm 114
Tremble, O earth, at the presence of the LORD. (Ps. 114:7)

Gospel
A Matthew 28:1–10
B Mark 16:1–8
C Luke 24:1–12

Verse
Alleluia. Christ being raised from the dead will never die again; death has no more dominion over him. Alleluia. Let us sing to the Lord who has triumphed gloriously. Alleluia. (Rom. 6:9; Ex. 15:1)

Offertory
Alleluia, alleluia, alleluia. Clean out the old yeast so that you may be a new batch of dough. For Christ our paschal Lamb has been sacrificed. Therefore, let us celebrate the festival with the unleavened bread of sincerity and truth. Alleluia, alleluia, alleluia. (1 Cor. 5:7–8)

Preface: Easter
Color: White *or* Gold

EASTER

THE RESURRECTION OF OUR LORD
Easter Day

Prayer of the Day
O God, you gave your only Son to suffer death on the cross for our redemption, and by his glorious resurrection you delivered us from the power of death. Make us die every day to sin, so that we may live with him forever in the joy of the resurrection; through Jesus Christ our Lord, who lives and reigns with you and the Holy Spirit, one God, now and forever. (62)

or

Almighty God, through your only Son you overcame death and opened for us the gate of everlasting life. Give us your continual help; put good desires into our minds and bring them to full effect; through Jesus Christ our Lord, who lives and reigns with you and the Holy Spirit, one God, now and forever. (63)

A
Acts 10:34–43 *or* Jeremiah 31:1–6
Psalm 118:1–2, 14–24
On this day the LORD has acted; we will rejoice and be glad in it. (Ps. 118:24)
Colossians 3:1–4 *or* Acts 10:34–43
John 20:1–18 *or* Matthew 28:1–10

B
Acts 10:34–43 *or* Isaiah 25:6–9
Psalm 118:1–2, 14–24
On this day the LORD has acted; we will rejoice and be glad in it. (Ps. 118:24)
1 Corinthians 15:1–11 *or* Acts 10:34–43
John 20:1–18 *or* Mark 16:1–8

C
Acts 10:34–43 *or* Isaiah 65:17–25
Psalm 118:1–2, 14–24
On this day the LORD has acted; we will rejoice and be glad in it. (Ps. 118:24)
1 Corinthians 15:19–26 *or* Acts 10:34–43
John 20:1–18 *or* Luke 24:1–12

Verse
Alleluia. Christ being raised from the dead will never die again; death no longer has dominion over him. Alleluia. On this day the LORD has acted; we will rejoice and be glad in it. Alleluia. (Rom. 6:9; Ps. 118:24)

The Sequence hymn, LBW #137, may follow.

Offertory
Alleluia, alleluia, alleluia. Clean out the old yeast so that you may be a new batch of dough. For Christ our paschal Lamb has been sacrificed. Therefore, let us celebrate the festival with the unleavened bread of sincerity and truth. Alleluia, alleluia, alleluia. (1 Cor. 5:7–8)

Preface: Easter
Color: White *or* Gold

THE RESURRECTION OF OUR LORD
Easter Evening

Prayer of the Day
Almighty God, you give us the joy of celebrating our Lord's resurrection. Give us also the joys of life in your service, and bring us at last to the full joy of life eternal; through your Son, Jesus Christ our Lord, who lives and reigns with you and the Holy Spirit, one God, now and forever. (64)

A, B, C
Isaiah 25:6–9
Psalm 114
Hallelujah. (Ps. 114:1)
1 Corinthians 5:6b–8
Luke 24:13–49

Verse
Alleluia. Christ being raised from the dead will never die again; death no longer has dominion over him. Alleluia. Beginning with Moses and all the prophets, Jesus interpreted the things about himself in all the scriptures. Alleluia. (Rom. 6:9; Luke 24:27)

Offertory
Alleluia, alleluia, alleluia. The disciples said, The Lord has risen indeed, and he has appeared to Simon! Then they told what had happened on the road, and how Jesus had been made known to them in the breaking of bread. Alleluia, alleluia, alleluia. (Luke 24:34–35)

Preface: Easter
Color: White

SECOND SUNDAY OF EASTER

Prayer of the Day
Almighty God, with joy we celebrate the festival of our Lord's resurrection. Graciously help us to show the power of the resurrection in all that we say and do; through your Son, Jesus Christ our Lord, who lives and reigns with you and the Holy Spirit, one God, now and forever. (65)

A
Acts 2:14a, 22–32
Psalm 16
In your presence there is fullness of joy.
(Ps. 16:11)
1 Peter 1:3–9
John 20:19–31

B
Acts 4:32–35
Psalm 133
How good and pleasant it is to live together in unity. (Ps. 133:1)
1 John 1:1—2:2
John 20:19–31

C
Acts 5:27–32
Psalm 118:14–29 *or* Psalm 150
This is the LORD's doing and it is marvelous in our eyes. (Ps. 118:23) or *Let everything that has breath praise the LORD.* (Ps. 150:6)
Revelation 1:4–8
John 20:19–31

Verse
Alleluia. Christ being raised from the dead will never die again; death no longer has dominion over him. Alleluia. Blessed are those who have not seen and yet have come to believe. Alleluia. (Rom. 6:9; John 20:29)

Offertory
Alleluia, alleluia, alleluia. Rid yourselves of all malice, and all guile, insincerity, envy, and all slander. Like newborn infants, long for the pure, spiritual milk, so that by it you may grow into salvation—if indeed you have tasted that the Lord is good. Alleluia, alleluia, alleluia. (1 Peter 2:1–3)

Preface: Easter
Color: White

THIRD SUNDAY OF EASTER

Prayer of the Day
O God, by the humiliation of your Son you lifted up this fallen world, rescuing us from the hopelessness of death. Grant your faithful people a share in the joys that are eternal; through your Son, Jesus Christ our Lord, who lives and reigns with you and the Holy Spirit, one God, now and forever. (66)

A
Acts 2:14a, 36–41
Psalm 116:1–3, 10–17*
I will call upon the name of the LORD.
(Ps. 116:11)
1 Peter 1:17–23
Luke 24:13–35

B
Acts 3:12–19
Psalm 4
The LORD does wonders for the faithful.
(Ps. 4:3)
1 John 3:1–7
Luke 24:36b–48

C
Acts 9:1–6 [7–20]
Psalm 30
You have turned my wailing into dancing.
(Ps. 30:12)
Revelation 5:11–14
John 21:1–19

Verse
Alleluia. Christ being raised from the dead will never die again; death no longer has dominion over him. Alleluia. Our hearts burn within us while he opens to us the scriptures. (Rom. 6:9; Luke 24:32)

Offertory
Alleluia, alleluia, alleluia. Christ is the image of the invisible God, the firstborn of all creation; for in him all things were created. He is the head of the body, the Church; he is the beginning, the firstborn from the dead. For in him all the fullness of God was pleased to dwell, and through him God was pleased to reconcile to himself all things, whether on earth or in heaven, by making peace through the blood of his cross. Alleluia, alleluia, alleluia. (Col. 1:15–20)

Preface: Easter
Color: White

*Psalm 116:1–4, 12–19 (NRSV)

FOURTH SUNDAY OF EASTER

Prayer of the Day

God of all power, you called from death our
Lord Jesus, the great shepherd of the sheep.
Send us as shepherds to rescue the lost, to
heal the injured, and to feed one another
with knowledge and understanding; through
your Son, Jesus Christ our Lord, who lives
and reigns with you and the Holy Spirit,
one God, now and forever. (67)

or

Almighty God, you show the light of your
truth to those in darkness, to lead them into
the way of righteousness. Give strength to all
who are joined in the family of the Church,
so that they will resolutely reject what erodes
their faith and firmly follow what faith
requires; through your Son, Jesus Christ our
Lord, who lives and reigns with you and the
Holy Spirit, one God, now and forever. (68)

A
Acts 2:42–47
Psalm 23
*The LORD is my shepherd; I shall not be in
want. (Ps. 23:1)*
1 Peter 2:19–25
John 10:1–10

B
Acts 4:5–12
Psalm 23
*The LORD is my shepherd; I shall not be in
want. (Ps. 23:1)*
1 John 3:16–24
John 10:11–18

C
Acts 9:36–43
Psalm 23
*The LORD is my shepherd; I shall not be in
want. (Ps. 23:1)*
Revelation 7:9–17
John 10:22–30

Verse

Alleluia. Christ being raised from the dead
will never die again; death no longer has
dominion over him. Alleluia. I am the good
shepherd. I know my own and my own
know me. Alleluia. (Rom. 6:9; John 10:14)

Offertory

Alleluia, alleluia, alleluia. Thus says the Lord
GOD: I myself will search for my sheep, and
will seek them out. As shepherds seek out
their flocks when they are among their
scattered sheep, so I will seek out my sheep.
I will bring them out from the peoples, and I
will feed them on the mountains of Israel.
Alleluia, alleluia, alleluia. (Ezek. 34:11–13)

Preface: Easter
Color: White

FIFTH SUNDAY OF EASTER

Prayer of the Day

O God, form the minds of your faithful
people into a single will. Make us love what
you command and desire what you promise,
that, amid all the changes of this world, our
hearts may be fixed where true joy is found;
through your Son, Jesus Christ our Lord,
who lives and reigns with you and the Holy
Spirit, one God, now and forever. (69)

A
Acts 7:55–60
Psalm 31:1–5, 15–16
*Into your hands, O LORD, I commend my
spirit. (Ps. 31:5)*
1 Peter 2:2–10
John 14:1–14

B
Acts 8:26–40
Psalm 22:24–30*
*All the ends of the earth shall remember and
turn to the LORD. (Ps. 22:26)*
1 John 4:7–21
John 15:1–8

C
Acts 11:1–18
Psalm 148
*The splendor of the LORD is over earth and
heaven. (Ps. 148:13)*
Revelation 21:1–6
John 13:31–35

Verse

Alleluia. Christ being raised from the dead
will never die again; death no longer has
dominion over him. Jesus said, I am the way,
and the truth, and the life. Alleluia.
(Rom. 6:9; John 14:6)

Offertory

Alleluia, alleluia, alleluia. Give thanks to
the LORD, call on his name; make known his
deeds among the nations; proclaim that his
name is exalted. Sing praises to the LORD,
for he has done gloriously; let this be known

in all the earth. Shout aloud and sing for joy, O royal Zion, for great in your midst is the Holy One of Israel. Alleluia, alleluia, alleluia. (Isa. 12:4–6)

Preface: Easter
Color: White

Psalm 22:25–31 (NRSV)

SIXTH SUNDAY OF EASTER

Prayer of the Day
O God, from whom all good things come: Lead us by the inspiration of your Spirit to think those things which are right, and by your goodness help us to do them; through your Son, Jesus Christ our Lord, who lives and reigns with you and the Holy Spirit, one God, now and forever. (70)

A
Acts 17:22–31
Psalm 66:7–18*
Be joyful in God, all you lands. (Ps. 66:1)
1 Peter 3:13–22
John 14:15–21

B
Acts 10:44–48
Psalm 98
Shout with joy to the LORD, all you lands. (Ps. 98:5)
1 John 5:1–6
John 15:9–17

C
Acts 16:9–15
Psalm 67
Let the nations be glad and sing for joy. (Ps. 67:4)
Revelation 21:10, 22—22:5
John 14:23–29 *or* John 5:1–9

Verse
Alleluia. Christ being raised from the dead will never die again; death no longer has dominion over him. Alleluia. Those who love me will keep my word, and my Father will love them, and we will come to them and make our home with them. Alleluia. (Rom 6:9; John 14:23)

Offertory
Alleluia, alleluia, alleluia. Very truly, I tell you, the one who believes in me will also do the works that I do and, in fact, will do

greater works than these, because I am going to the Father. I will do whatever you ask in my name, so that the Father may be glorified in the Son. If in my name you ask me for anything, I will do it. Alleluia, alleluia, alleluia. (John 14:12–14)

Preface: Easter
Color: White

Psalm 66:8–20 (NRSV)

THE ASCENSION OF OUR LORD

Prayer of the Day
Almighty God, your only Son was taken up into heaven and in power intercedes for us. May we also come into your presence and live forever in your glory; through your Son, Jesus Christ our Lord, who lives and reigns with you and the Holy Spirit, one God, now and forever. (71)

A
Acts 1:1–11
Psalm 47 *or* Psalm 93
God has gone up with a shout. (Ps. 47:5)
or *Ever since the world began, your throne has been established. (Ps. 93:3)*
Ephesians 1:15–23
Luke 24:44–53

B
Acts 1:1–11
Psalm 47 *or* Psalm 93
God has gone up with a shout. (Ps. 47:5)
or *Ever since the world began, your throne has been established. (Ps. 93:3)*
Ephesians 1:15–23
Luke 24:44–53

C
Acts 1:1–11
Psalm 47 *or* Psalm 93
God has gone up with a shout. (Ps. 47:5)
or *Ever since the world began, your throne has been established. (Ps. 93:3)*
Ephesians 1:15–23
Luke 24:44–53

Verse
Alleluia. Christ being raised from the dead will never die again; death no longer has dominion over him. Alleluia. I am with you always, to the end of the age. Alleluia. (Rom. 6:9; Matt. 28:20)

Offertory

Alleluia, alleluia, alleluia. I saw one like a human being coming with the clouds of heaven. And he came to the Ancient One and was presented before him. To him was given dominion and glory and kingship, that all peoples, nations, and languages should serve him. His dominion is an everlasting dominion that shall not pass away, and his kingship is one that shall never be destroyed. Alleluia, alleluia, alleluia. (Dan. 7:13–14)

Preface: Ascension
Color: White

SEVENTH SUNDAY OF EASTER

Prayer of the Day

Almighty and eternal God, your Son our Savior is with you in eternal glory. Give us faith to see that, true to his promise, he is among us still, and will be with us to the end of time; who lives and reigns with you and the Holy Spirit, one God, now and forever. (72)

or

God, our creator and redeemer, your Son Jesus prayed that his followers might be one. Make all Christians one with him as he is one with you, so that in peace and concord we may carry to the world the message of your love; through Jesus Christ our Lord, who lives and reigns with you and the Holy Spirit, one God, now and forever. (73)

A

Acts 1:6–14
Psalm 68:1–10, 33–36*
Sing to God, who rides upon the heavens.
(Ps. 68:4)
1 Peter 4:12–14; 5:6–11
John 17:1–11

B

Acts 1:15–17, 21–26
Psalm 1
The LORD knows the way of the righteous.
(Ps. 1:6)
1 John 5:9–13
John 17:6–19

C

Acts 16:16–34
Psalm 97
Rejoice in the LORD, you righteous. (Ps. 97:12)
Revelation 22:12–14, 16–17, 20–21
John 17:20–26

Verse

Alleluia. Christ being raised from the dead will never die again; death no longer has dominion over him. Alleluia. I will not leave you orphaned; I am coming to you. Alleluia. (Rom. 6:9; John 14:18)

Offertory

Alleluia, alleluia, alleluia. Ask, and it will be given you; search, and you will find; knock, and the door will be opened for you. Is there anyone among you who, if your child asks for bread, will give a stone? If you then know how to give good gifts to your children, how much more will your Father in heaven give good things to those who ask him! Alleluia, alleluia, alleluia. (Matt. 7:7, 9, 11)

Preface: Ascension
Color: White

Psalm 68:1–10, 32–35 (NRSV)

VIGIL OF PENTECOST

Prayer of the Day

Almighty and ever-living God, you fulfilled the promise of Easter by sending your Holy Spirit to unite the races and nations on earth and thus to proclaim your glory. Look upon your people gathered in prayer, open to receive the Spirit's flame. May it come to rest in our hearts and heal the divisions of word and tongue, that with one voice and one song we may praise your name in joy and thanksgiving; through your Son, Jesus Christ our Lord, who lives and reigns with you and the Holy Spirit, one God, now and forever. (74)

A, B, C

Exodus 19:1–9 *or* Acts 2:1–11
Psalm 33:12–22 *or* Psalm 130
The LORD is our help and our shield. (Ps. 33:20)
or *There is forgiveness with you. (Ps. 130:3)*
Romans 8:14–17, 22–27
John 7:37–39

Verse

Alleluia. Come, Holy Spirit, fill the hearts of your faithful people; set them on fire with your love. Alleluia.

Offertory

Be careful then how you live, not as unwise people but as wise. Be filled with the Spirit, as you sing psalms and hymns and spiritual songs among yourselves, singing and making melody to the Lord in your hearts, giving thanks to God the Father at all times and for everything in the name of our Lord Jesus Christ. (Eph. 5:15, 18–20)

Preface: Pentecost
Color: Red

THE DAY OF PENTECOST

Prayer of the Day

God, the Father of our Lord Jesus Christ, as you sent upon the disciples the promised gift of the Holy Spirit, look upon your Church and open our hearts to the power of the Spirit. Kindle in us the fire of your love, and strengthen our lives for service in your kingdom; through your Son, Jesus Christ our Lord, who lives and reigns with you in the unity of the Holy Spirit, one God, now and forever. (75)

or (Year C)

God our creator, earth has many languages, but your Gospel announces your love to all nations in one heavenly speech. Make us messengers of the good news that, through the power of your Spirit, everyone everywhere may unite in one song of praise; through your Son, Jesus Christ our Lord, who lives and reigns with you in the unity of the Holy Spirit, one God, now and forever. (76)

A

Acts 2:1–21 *or* Numbers 11:24–30
Psalm 104:25–35, 37*
Alleluia, or *Send forth your Spirit and renew the face of the earth. (Ps. 104:31)*
1 Corinthians 12:3b–13 *or* Acts 2:1–21
John 20:19–23 *or* John 7:37–39

B

Acts 2:1–21 *or* Ezekiel 37:1–14
Psalm 104:25–35, 37*
Alleluia, or *Send forth your Spirit and renew the face of the earth. (Ps. 104:31)*
Romans 8:22–27 *or* Acts 2:1–21
John 15:26–27; 16:4b–15

C

Acts 2:1–21 *or* Genesis 11:1–9
Psalm 104:25–35, 37*
Alleluia, or *Send forth your Spirit and renew the face of the earth. (Ps. 104:31)*
Romans 8:14–17 *or* Acts 2:1–21
John 14:8–17 [25–27]

Verse

Alleluia. Come, Holy Spirit, fill the hearts of your faithful people; set them on fire with your love. Alleluia.

The Sequence hymn, LBW #472, may follow.

Offertory

Be careful then how you live, not as unwise people but as wise. Be filled with the Spirit, as you sing psalms and hymns and spiritual songs among yourselves, singing and making melody to the Lord in your hearts, giving thanks to God the Father at all times and for everything in the name of our Lord Jesus Christ. (Eph. 5:15, 18–20)

Preface: Pentecost
Color: Red

*Psalm 104:24–34, 35b (NRSV)

SUNDAYS AFTER PENTECOST

THE HOLY TRINITY
First Sunday after Pentecost

Prayer of the Day
Almighty God our Father, dwelling in majesty and mystery, renewing and fulfilling creation by your eternal Spirit, and revealing your glory through our Lord, Jesus Christ: Cleanse us from doubt and fear, and enable us to worship you, with your Son and the Holy Spirit, one God, living and reigning, now and forever. (77)

or
Almighty and ever-living God, you have given us grace, by the confession of the true faith, to acknowledge the glory of the eternal Trinity and, in the power of your divine majesty, to worship the unity. Keep us steadfast in this faith and worship, and bring us at last to see you in your eternal glory, one God, now and forever. (78)

A
Genesis 1:1—2:4a
Psalm 8
How exalted is your name in all the world!
(Ps. 8:1)
2 Corinthians 13:11–13
Matthew 28:16–20

B
Isaiah 6:1–8
Psalm 29
Worship the LORD in the beauty of holiness.
(Ps. 29:2)
Romans 8:12–17
John 3:1–17

C
Proverbs 8:1–4, 22–31
Psalm 8
Your majesty is praised above the heavens.
(Ps. 8:2)
Romans 5:1–5
John 16:12–15

Verse
Alleluia. Holy, holy, holy is the LORD of hosts; the whole earth is full of his glory. Alleluia. (Isa. 6:3)

Offertory
Great and amazing are your deeds, Lord God the Almighty! Just and true are your ways, King of the nations! Lord, who will not fear and glorify your name? For you alone are holy. All nations will come and worship you, for your judgments have been revealed. (Rev. 15:3–4)

Preface: The Holy Trinity
Color: White

MAY 24 AND 28 INCLUSIVE
(if after Trinity Sunday)
Proper 3

Prayer of the Day
Almighty and everlasting God, ruler of heaven and earth: Hear our prayer and give us your peace now and forever; through your Son, Jesus Christ our Lord. (19)

A
Isaiah 49:8–16a
Psalm 131
Like a child upon its mother's breast, my soul is quieted within me. (Ps. 131:3)
1 Corinthians 4:1–5
Matthew 6:24–34

B
Hosea 2:14–20
Psalm 103:1–13, 22
The LORD is full of compassion and mercy.
(Ps. 103:8)
2 Corinthians 3:1–6
Mark 2:13–22

C
Isaiah 55:10–13 (*or* Sirach 27:4–7)
Psalm 92:1–4, 11–14*
The righteous shall flourish like a palm tree.
(Ps. 92:11)
1 Corinthians 15:51–58
Luke 6:39–49

Verse
Alleluia. The steadfast love of the LORD never ceases; his mercies never come to an end. Alleluia. (Lam. 3:22)

Offertory
I put my trust in your mercy; my heart is joyful because of your saving help. I will sing to you, O LORD, for you have dealt with me richly. (Ps. 13:5–6)

Preface: Sundays after Pentecost
Color: Green

*Psalm 92:1–4, 12–15 (NRSV)

SUNDAY BETWEEN
MAY 29 AND JUNE 4 INCLUSIVE
(if after Trinity Sunday)
Proper 4

Prayer of the Day
Lord God of all nations, you have revealed
your will to your people and promised your
help to us all. Help us to hear and to do
what you command, that the darkness may
be overcome by the power of your light;
through your Son, Jesus Christ our Lord. (79)

A
Deuteronomy 11:18–21, 26–28
Psalm 31:1–5, 19–24
Be my strong rock, a castle to keep me safe.
(Ps. 31:3)
Romans 1:16–17; 3:22b–28 [29–31]
Matthew 7:21–29

B
Deuteronomy 5:12–15
Psalm 81:1–10
Raise a loud shout to the God of Jacob.
(Ps. 81:1)
2 Corinthians 4:5–12
Mark 2:23—3:6

C
1 Kings 8:22–23, 41–43
Psalm 96:1–9
Declare the glory of the LORD among the
nations. (Ps. 96:3)
Galatians 1:1–12
Luke 7:1–10

Verse
Alleluia. Your word is a lantern to my feet
and a light upon my path. Alleluia.
(Ps. 119:105)

Offertory
The steadfast love of the LORD never
ceases, his mercies never come to an end;
they are new every morning; great is your
faithfulness. "The LORD is my portion," says
my soul, "therefore I will hope in him."
(Lam. 3:22–24)

Preface: Sundays after Pentecost
Color: Green

SUNDAY BETWEEN
JUNE 5 AND 11 INCLUSIVE
(if after Trinity Sunday)
Proper 5

Prayer of the Day
O God, the strength of those who hope in
you: Be present and hear our prayers; and,
because in the weakness of our mortal
nature we can do nothing good without
you, give us the help of your grace, so that
in keeping your commandments we may
please you in will and deed; through your
Son, Jesus Christ our Lord. (80)

A
Hosea 5:15—6:6
Psalm 50:7–15
To those who keep in my way will I show the
salvation of God. (Ps. 50:24)
Romans 4:13–25
Matthew 9:9–13, 18–26

B
Genesis 3:8–15
Psalm 130
With the LORD there is mercy and plenteous
redemption. (Ps. 130:7)
2 Corinthians 4:13—5:1
Mark 3:20–35

C
1 Kings 17:17–24
Psalm 30
My God, I cried out to you, and you restored
me to health. (Ps. 30:2)
Galatians 1:11–24
Luke 7:11–17

Verse
Alleluia. In Christ God was reconciling
the world to himself, and entrusting the
message of reconciliation to us. Alleluia.
(2 Cor. 5:19)

Offertory
They devoted themselves to the apostles'
teaching and fellowship, to the breaking of
bread and the prayers. Day by day, as they
spent much time together in the temple,
they broke bread at home and ate their
food with glad and generous hearts.
(Acts 2:42, 46)

Preface: Sundays after Pentecost
Color: Green

SUNDAY BETWEEN
JUNE 12 AND 18 INCLUSIVE
(if after Trinity Sunday)
Proper 6

Prayer of the Day
God, our maker and redeemer, you have made us a new company of priests to bear witness to the Gospel. Enable us to be faithful to our calling to make known your promises to all the world; through your Son, Jesus Christ our Lord. (81)

A
Exodus 19:2–8a
Psalm 100
We are God's people and the sheep of God's pasture. (Ps. 100:2)
Romans 5:1–8
Matthew 9:35—10:8 [9–23]

B
Ezekiel 17:22–24
Psalm 92:1–4, 11–14*
The righteous shall spread abroad like a cedar of Lebanon. (Ps. 92:11)
2 Corinthians 5:6–10 [11–13] 14–17
Mark 4:26–34

C
2 Samuel 11:26—12:10, 13–15
Psalm 32
Then you forgave me the guilt of my sin. (Ps. 32:6)
Galatians 2:15–21
Luke 7:36—8:3

Verse
Alleluia. Let your priests be clothed with righteousness; let your faithful people sing for joy. Alleluia. (Ps. 132:9)

Offertory
You are a chosen race, a royal priesthood, a holy nation, God's own people, in order that you may proclaim the mighty acts of him who called you out of darkness into his marvelous light. Once you were not a people, but now you are God's people; once you had not received mercy, but now you have received mercy. (1 Peter 2:9–10)

Preface: Sundays after Pentecost
Color: Green

*Psalm 92:1–4, 12–15 (NRSV)

SUNDAY BETWEEN
JUNE 19 AND 25 INCLUSIVE
(if after Trinity Sunday)
Proper 7

Prayer of the Day
O God our defender, storms rage about us and cause us to be afraid. Rescue your people from despair, deliver your sons and daughters from fear, and preserve us all from unbelief; through your Son, Jesus Christ our Lord. (82)

A
Jeremiah 20:7–13
Psalm 69:8–11 [12–17] 18–20*
Answer me, O LORD, for your love is kind. (Ps. 69:18)
Romans 6:1b–11
Matthew 10:24–39

B
Job 38:1–11
Psalm 107:1–3, 23–32
God stilled the storm and quieted the waves of the sea. (Ps. 107:29)
2 Corinthians 6:1–13
Mark 4:35–41

C
Isaiah 65:1–9
Psalm 22:18–27**
In the midst of the congregation I will praise you. (Ps. 22:21)
Galatians 3:23–29
Luke 8:26–39

Verse
Alleluia. Because you are children, God has sent the Spirit of his Son into your hearts, crying, "Abba! Father!" Alleluia. (Gal. 4:6)

Offertory
The LORD is faithful in all his words and merciful in all his deeds. The LORD upholds all those who fall; he lifts up those who are bowed down. The eyes of all wait upon you, O LORD, and you give them their food in due season. You open wide your hand and satisfy the needs of every living creature. (Ps. 145:14–17)

Preface: Sundays after Pentecost
Color: Green

*Psalm 69:7–10 (11–15) 16–18 (NRSV)
**Psalm 22:19–28 (NRSV)

SUNDAY BETWEEN
JUNE 26 AND JULY 2 INCLUSIVE
Proper 8

Prayer of the Day
O God, you have prepared for those
who love you joys beyond understanding.
Pour into our hearts such love for you that,
loving you above all things, we may obtain
your promises, which exceed all that we can
desire; through your Son, Jesus Christ our
Lord. (83)

A
Jeremiah 28:5–9
Psalm 89:1–4, 15–18
Your love, O LORD, forever will I sing.
(Ps. 89:1)
Romans 6:12–23
Matthew 10:40–42

B
Lamentations 3:22–33
(*or* Wisdom of Solomon 1:13–15; 2:23–24)
Psalm 30
I will exalt you, O LORD, because you have
lifted me up. (Ps. 30:1)
2 Corinthians 8:7–15
Mark 5:21–43

C
1 Kings 19:15–16, 19–21
Psalm 16
I have set the LORD always before me.
(Ps. 16:8)
Galatians 5:1, 13–25
Luke 9:51–62

Verse
Alleluia. May the God of our Lord Jesus
Christ enlighten the eyes of our hearts that
we may know the hope to which he has
called us. Alleluia. (Eph. 1:17)

Offertory
The LORD is the strength of my life; of
whom then shall I be afraid? I believe that
I shall see the goodness of the LORD in the
land of the living! I will offer in his dwelling
an oblation with sounds of great gladness;
I will sing and make music to the LORD.
(Ps. 27:1, 17, 9)

Preface: Sundays after Pentecost
Color: Green

SUNDAY BETWEEN
JULY 3 AND 9 INCLUSIVE
Proper 9

Prayer of the Day
God of glory and love, peace comes from
you alone. Send us as peacemakers and
witnesses to your kingdom, and fill our
hearts with joy in your promises of salvation; through your Son, Jesus Christ our
Lord. (84)

A
Zechariah 9:9–12
Psalm 145:8–15*
*The LORD is gracious and full of compas-
sion. (Ps. 145:8)*
Romans 7:15–25a
Matthew 11:16–19, 25–30

B
Ezekiel 2:1–5
Psalm 123
*Our eyes look to you, O God, until you
show us your mercy. (Ps. 123:3)*
2 Corinthians 12:2–10
Mark 6:1–13

C
Isaiah 66:10–14
Psalm 66:1–8**
God holds our souls in life. (Ps. 66:8)
Galatians 6:[1–6] 7–16
Luke 10:1–11, 16–20

Verse
Alleluia. Happy are they who hear the
word, hold it fast in an honest and good
heart, and bear fruit with patient
endurance. Alleluia. (Luke 8:15)

Offertory
Come to me, all you that are weary and are
carrying heavy burdens, and I will give you
rest. Take my yoke upon you, and learn
from me; for I am gentle and humble in
heart, and you will find rest for your souls.
For my yoke is easy, and my burden is light.
(Matt. 11:28–30)

Preface: Sundays after Pentecost
Color: Green

*Psalm 145:8–14 (NRSV)
**Psalm 66:1–9 (NRSV)

SUNDAY BETWEEN
JULY 10 AND 16 INCLUSIVE
Proper 10

Prayer of the Day
Almighty God, we thank you for planting in us the seed of your word. By your Holy Spirit help us to receive it with joy, live according to it, and grow in faith and hope and love; through your Son, Jesus Christ our Lord. (85)

or (Year C)
Lord God, use our lives to touch the world with your love. Stir us, by your Spirit, to be neighbor to those in need, serving them with willing hearts; through your Son, Jesus Christ our Lord. (86)

A
Isaiah 55:10–13
Psalm 65:[1–8] 9–14*
Your paths overflow with plenty. (Ps. 65:12)
Romans 8:1–11
Matthew 13:1–9, 18–23

B
Amos 7:7–15
Psalm 85:8–13
*I will listen to what the LORD God is saying.
(Ps. 85:8)*
Ephesians 1:3–14
Mark 6:14–29

C
Deuteronomy 30:9–14
Psalm 25:1–9**
Show me your ways, O LORD, and teach me your paths. (Ps. 25:3)
Colossians 1:1–14
Luke 10:25–37

Verse
Alleluia. The word is very near to you; it is in your mouth and in your heart for you to observe. Alleluia. (Deut. 30:14)

Offertory
Jesus said, "The first commandment is: 'Hear, O Israel: the Lord our God, the Lord is one; you shall love the Lord your God with all your heart, and with all your soul, and with all your mind, and with all your strength.' The second is this: 'You shall love your neighbor as yourself.' " (Mark 12:29–31)

Preface: Sundays after Pentecost
Color: Green

*Psalm 65:[1–8] 9–13 (NRSV)
**Psalm 25:1–10 (NRSV)

SUNDAY BETWEEN
JULY 17 AND 23 INCLUSIVE
Proper 11

Prayer of the Day
O Lord, pour out upon us the spirit to think and do what is right, that we, who cannot even exist without you, may have the strength to live according to your will; through your Son, Jesus Christ our Lord. (87)

or (Year C)
O God, you see how busy we are with many things. Turn us to listen to your teachings and lead us to choose the one thing which will not be taken from us, Jesus Christ our Lord. (88)

A
Isaiah 44:6–8
(*or* Wisdom of Solomon 12:13, 16–19)
Psalm 86:11–17
Teach me your way, O LORD, and I will walk in your truth. (Ps. 86:11)
Romans 8:12–25
Matthew 13:24–30, 36–43

B
Jeremiah 23:1–6
Psalm 23
The LORD is my shepherd; I shall not be in want. (Ps. 23:1)
Ephesians 2:11–22
Mark 6:30–34, 53–56

C
Genesis 18:1–10a
Psalm 15
Who may abide upon your holy hill? Whoever leads a blameless life and does what is right. (Ps. 15:1–2)
Colossians 1:15–28
Luke 10:38–42

Verse
Alleluia. My word shall accomplish that which I purpose, and succeed in the thing for which I sent it. Alleluia. (Isa. 55:11)

Offertory
I will wash my hands in innocence, O LORD, that I may go in procession round your altar, singing aloud a song of thanksgiving and recounting all your wonderful deeds. LORD, I love the house in which you dwell and the place where your glory abides. (Ps. 26:6–8)

Preface: Sundays after Pentecost
Color: Green

SUNDAY BETWEEN
JULY 24 AND 30 INCLUSIVE
Proper 12

Prayer of the Day
O God, your ears are open always to the prayers of your servants. Open our hearts and minds to you, that we may live in harmony with your will and receive the gifts of your Spirit; through your Son, Jesus Christ our Lord. (89)

A

1 Kings 3:5–12
Psalm 119:129–136
When your word goes forth, it gives light and understanding. (Ps. 119:130)
Romans 8:26–39
Matthew 13:31–33, 44–52

B

2 Kings 4:42–44
Psalm 145:10–19*
You open wide your hand and satisfy the needs of every living creature. (Ps. 145:17)
Ephesians 3:14–21
John 6:1–21

C

Genesis 18:20–32
Psalm 138
Your love endures forever; do not abandon the works of your hands. (Ps. 138:9)
Colossians 2:6–15 [16–19]
Luke 11:1–13

Verse
Alleluia. Lord, to whom shall we go? You have the words of eternal life. Alleluia. (John 6:68)

Offertory
The sparrow has found her a house and the swallow a nest where she may lay her young, by the side of your altars, O LORD of hosts, my King and my God. Happy are they who dwell in your house! They will always be praising you. (Ps. 84:2–3)

Preface: Sundays after Pentecost
Color: Green

Psalm 145:10–18 (NRSV)

SUNDAY BETWEEN JULY 31 AND
AUGUST 6 INCLUSIVE
Proper 13

Prayer of the Day
Gracious Father, your blessed Son came down from heaven to be the true bread which gives life to the world. Give us this bread, that he may live in us and we in him, Jesus Christ our Lord. (90)

or (Year C)
Almighty God, judge of us all, you have placed in our hands the wealth we call our own. Give us such wisdom by your Spirit that our possessions may not be a curse in our lives, but an instrument for blessing; through your Son, Jesus Christ our Lord. (91)

A

Isaiah 55:1–5
Psalm 145:8–9, 15–22*
You open wide your hand and satisfy the needs of every living creature. (Ps. 145:17)
Romans 9:1–5
Matthew 14:13–21

B

Exodus 16:2–4, 9–15
Psalm 78:23–29
The LORD rained down manna upon them to eat. (Ps. 78:24)
Ephesians 4:1–16
John 6:24–35

C

Ecclesiastes 1:2, 12–14; 2:18–23
Psalm 49:1–11**
We can never ransom ourselves or deliver to God the price of our life. (Ps. 49:6)
Colossians 3:1–11
Luke 12:13–21

Verse
Alleluia. Jesus said, Those who love me will keep my word, and my Father will love them, and we will come to them and make our home with them. Alleluia. (John 14:23)

Offertory
Honor the LORD with your substance and with the first fruits of all your produce; then your barns will be filled with plenty, and your vats will be bursting with wine. (Prov. 3:9–10)

Preface: Sundays after Pentecost
Color: Green

Psalm 145:8–9, 14–21 (NRSV)
**Psalm 49:1–12 (NRSV)*

SUNDAY BETWEEN
AUGUST 7 AND 13 INCLUSIVE
Proper 14

Prayer of the Day
Almighty and everlasting God, you are always more ready to hear than we are to pray, and to give more than we either desire or deserve. Pour upon us the abundance of your mercy, forgiving us those things of which our conscience is afraid, and giving us those good things for which we are not worthy to ask, except through the merit of your Son, Jesus Christ our Lord. (92)

A
1 Kings 19:9–18
Psalm 85:8–13
I will listen to what the LORD God is saying. (Ps. 85:8)
Romans 10:5–15
Matthew 14:22–33

B
1 Kings 19:4–8
Psalm 34:1–8
Taste and see that the LORD is good. (Ps. 34:8)
Ephesians 4:25—5:2
John 6:35, 41–51

C
Genesis 15:1–6
Psalm 33:12–22
Let your lovingkindness be upon us, as we have put our trust in you. (Ps. 33:22)
Hebrews 11:1–3, 8–16
Luke 12:32–40

Verse
Alleluia. Faith is the assurance of things hoped for, the conviction of things not seen. Alleluia. (Heb. 11:1)

Offertory
The earth is fully satisfied by the fruit of your works. You make grass grow for flocks and herds, and plants to serve humankind; that they may bring forth food from the earth, and wine to gladden our hearts, oil to make a cheerful countenance, and bread to strengthen the heart. (Ps. 104:13–15)

Preface: Sundays after Pentecost
Color: Green

SUNDAY BETWEEN
AUGUST 14 AND 20 INCLUSIVE
Proper 15

Prayer of the Day
Almighty and ever-living God, you have given great and precious promises to those who believe. Grant us the perfect faith which overcomes all doubts, through your Son, Jesus Christ our Lord. (93)

A
Isaiah 56:1, 6–8
Psalm 67
Let all the peoples praise you, O God. (Ps. 67:3)
Romans 11:1–2a, 29–32
Matthew 15:[10–20] 21–28

B
Proverbs 9:1–6
Psalm 34:9–14
Those who seek the LORD lack nothing that is good. (Ps. 34:10)
Ephesians 5:15–20
John 6:51–58

C
Jeremiah 23:23–29
Psalm 82
Arise, O God, and rule the earth. (Ps. 82:8)
Hebrews 11:29—12:2
Luke 12:49–56

Verse
Alleluia. The Word of God is living and active, sharper than any two-edged sword, able to judge the thoughts and intentions of the heart. Alleluia. (Heb. 4:12)

Offertory
Ascribe to the LORD, O families of the peoples, ascribe to the LORD glory and strength! Ascribe to the LORD the glory due his name; bring an offering and come before him. Worship the LORD in holy splendor. Oh, give thanks to the LORD, for he is good; for his steadfast love endures forever. (1 Chron. 16:28–29, 34)

Preface: Sundays after Pentecost
Color: Green

SUNDAY BETWEEN AUGUST 21 AND 27 INCLUSIVE
Proper 16

Prayer of the Day
God of all creation, you reach out to call people of all nations to your kingdom. As you gather disciples from near and far, count us also among those who boldly confess your Son Jesus Christ as Lord. (94)

A
Isaiah 51:1–6
Psalm 138
O LORD, your love endures forever. (Ps. 138:9)
Romans 12:1–8
Matthew 16:13–20

B
Joshua 24:1–2a, 14–18
Psalm 34:15–22
The eyes of the LORD are upon the righteous. (Ps. 34:15)
Ephesians 6:10–20
John 6:56–69

C
Isaiah 58:9b–14
Psalm 103:1–8
The LORD crowns you with mercy and lovingkindness. (Ps. 103:4)
Hebrews 12:18–29
Luke 13:10–17

Verse
Alleluia. Our Savior Jesus Christ abolished death and brought life and immortality to light through the gospel. Alleluia. (2 Tim. 1:10)

Offertory
Do not worry, saying "What will we eat?" or "What will we drink?" or "What will we wear?" Your heavenly Father knows that you need all these things. But strive first for the kingdom of God and its righteousness, and all these things will be given to you as well. (Matt. 6:31–33)

Preface: Sundays after Pentecost
Color: Green

SUNDAY BETWEEN AUGUST 28 AND SEPTEMBER 3 INCLUSIVE
Proper 17

Prayer of the Day
O God, we thank you for your Son who chose the path of suffering for the sake of the world. Humble us by his example, point us to the path of obedience, and give us strength to follow his commands; through your Son, Jesus Christ our Lord. (95)

A
Jeremiah 15:15–21
Psalm 26:1–8
Your love is before my eyes; I have walked faithfully with you. (Ps. 26:3)
Romans 12:9–21
Matthew 16:21–28

B
Deuteronomy 4:1–2, 6–9
Psalm 15
LORD, who may dwell in your tabernacle? (Ps. 15:1)
James 1:17–27
Mark 7:1–8, 14–15, 21–23

C
Proverbs 25:6–7 (*or* Sirach 10:12–18)
Psalm 112
The righteous are merciful and full of compassion. (Ps. 112:4)
Hebrews 13:1–8, 15–16
Luke 14:1, 7–14

Verse
Alleluia. Your words became to me a joy, and the delight of my heart. Alleluia. (Jer. 15:16)

Offertory
This is the bread that comes down from heaven, so that one may eat of it and not die. I am the living bread that came down from heaven. Whoever eats of this bread will live forever; and the bread that I will give for the life of the world is my flesh. (John 6:50–51)

Preface: Sundays after Pentecost
Color: Green

SUNDAY BETWEEN
SEPTEMBER 4 AND 10 INCLUSIVE
Proper 18

Prayer of the Day
Almighty and eternal God, you know our problems and our weaknesses better than we ourselves. In your love and by your power help us in our confusion and, in spite of our weakness, make us firm in faith; through your Son, Jesus Christ our Lord. (96)

A
Ezekiel 33:7–11
Psalm 119:33–40
I desire the path of your commandments.
(Ps. 119:35)
Romans 13:8–14
Matthew 18:15–20

B
Isaiah 35:4–7a
Psalm 146
I will praise the LORD as long as I live.
(Ps. 146:1)
James 2:1–10 [11–13] 14–17
Mark 7:24–37

C
Deuteronomy 30:15–20
Psalm 1
Their delight is in the law of the LORD. (Ps. 1:2)
Philemon 1–21
Luke 14:25–33

Verse
Alleluia. Rejoice in the Lord always; again I will say, Rejoice. Alleluia. (Phil. 4:4)

Offertory
Do not lag in zeal, be ardent in spirit, serve the Lord. Rejoice in hope, be patient in suffering, persevere in prayer. Contribute to the needs of the saints; extend hospitality to strangers. (Rom. 12:11–13)

Preface: Sundays after Pentecost
Color: Green

SUNDAY BETWEEN
SEPTEMBER 11 AND 17 INCLUSIVE
Proper 19

Prayer of the Day
O God, you declare your almighty power chiefly in showing mercy and pity. Grant us the fullness of your grace, that, pursuing what you have promised, we may share your heavenly glory; through your Son, Jesus Christ our Lord. (97)

A
Genesis 50:15–21
Psalm 103:[1–7] 8–13
The LORD is full of compassion and mercy.
(Ps. 103:8)
Romans 14:1–12
Matthew 18:21–35

B
Isaiah 50:4–9a
Psalm 116:1–8*
I will walk in the presence of the LORD.
(Ps. 116:8)
James 3:1–12
Mark 8:27–38

C
Exodus 32:7–14
Psalm 51:1–11**
Have mercy on me, O God, according to your lovingkindness. (Ps. 51:1)
1 Timothy 1:12–17
Luke 15:1–10

Verse
Alleluia. Whatever was written in former days was written for our instruction, so that by steadfastness and by the encouragement of the scriptures we might have hope. Alleluia. (Rom. 15:4)

Offertory
Those who observe the day, observe it in honor of the Lord. Also those who eat, eat in honor of the Lord. We do not live to ourselves, and we do not die to ourselves. If we live, we live to the Lord, and if we die, we die to the Lord; so then, whether we live or whether we die, we are the Lord's. (Rom. 14:6–8)

Preface: Sundays after Pentecost
Color: Green

*Psalm 116:1–9 (NRSV)
**Psalm 51:1–10 (NRSV)

SUNDAY BETWEEN SEPTEMBER 18 AND 24 INCLUSIVE
Proper 20

Prayer of the Day
Lord God, you call us to work in your vine-yard and leave no one standing idle. Set us to our tasks in the work of your kingdom, and help us to order our lives by your wisdom; through your Son, Jesus Christ our Lord. (98)

A
Jonah 3:10—4:11
Psalm 145:1–8
The LORD is slow to anger and of great kindness. (Ps. 145:8)
Philippians 1:21–30
Matthew 20:1–16

B
Jeremiah 11:18–20
(*or* Wisdom of Solomon 1:16—2:1, 12–22)
Psalm 54
God is my helper; it is the LORD who sustains my life. (Ps. 54:4)
James 3:13—4:3, 7–8a
Mark 9:30–37

C
Amos 8:4–7
Psalm 113
The LORD lifts up the poor from the ashes. (Ps. 113:6)
1 Timothy 2:1–7
Luke 16:1–13

Verse
Alleluia. Live your life in a manner worthy of the gospel of Christ; strive side by side for the faith of the Gospel. Alleluia. (Phil. 1:27)

Offertory
I am the true vine, and my Father is the vinegrower. Abide in me as I abide in you. Just as the branch cannot bear fruit by itself unless it abides in the vine, neither can you unless you abide in me. I am the vine, you are the branches. Those who abide in me and I in them bear much fruit. (John 15:1, 4–5)

Preface: Sundays after Pentecost
Color: Green

SUNDAY BETWEEN SEPTEMBER 25 AND OCTOBER 1 INCLUSIVE
Proper 21

Prayer of the Day
God of love, you know our frailties and failings. Give us your grace to overcome them; keep us from those things that harm us; and guide us in the way of salvation; through your Son, Jesus Christ our Lord. (99)

A
Ezekiel 18:1–4, 25–32
Psalm 25:1–8*
Remember, O LORD, your compassion and love. (Ps. 25:5)
Philippians 2:1–13
Matthew 21:23–32

B
Numbers 11:4–6, 10–16, 24–29
Psalm 19:7–14
The commandment of the LORD gives light to the eyes. (Ps. 19:8)
James 5:13–20
Mark 9:38–50

C
Amos 6:1a, 4–7
Psalm 146
The LORD gives justice to those who are oppressed. (Ps. 146:6)
1 Timothy 6:6–19
Luke 16:19–31

Verse
Alleluia. At the name of Jesus every knee should bend, and every tongue should confess that Jesus Christ is Lord, to the glory of God the Father. Alleluia. (Phil. 2:10–11)

Offertory
Listen! I am standing at the door, knocking; if you hear my voice and open the door, I will come in to you and eat with you and you with me. To the one who conquers, I will give a place with me on my throne, just as I myself conquered and sat down with my Father on his throne. (Rev. 3:20–21)

Preface: Sundays after Pentecost
Color: Green

*Psalm 25:1–9 (NRSV)

SUNDAY BETWEEN
OCTOBER 2 AND 8 INCLUSIVE
Proper 22

Prayer of the Day
Our Lord Jesus, you have endured the doubts and foolish questions of every generation. Forgive us for trying to be judge over you, and grant us the confident faith to acknowledge you as Lord. (100)

A
Isaiah 5:1–7
Psalm 80:7–14*
Look down from heaven, O God; behold and tend this vine. (Ps. 80:14)
Philippians 3:4b–14
Matthew 21:33–46

B
Genesis 2:18–24
Psalm 8
You adorn us with glory and honor. (Ps. 8:6)
Hebrews 1:1–4; 2:5–12
Mark 10:2–16

C
Habakkuk 1:1–4; 2:1–4
Psalm 37:1–10**
Commit your way to the LORD; put your trust in the LORD. (Ps. 37:5)
2 Timothy 1:1–14
Luke 17:5–10

Verse
Alleluia. I will proclaim your name to my brothers and sisters; in the midst of the congregation I will praise you. Alleluia. (Heb. 2:12)

Offertory
Taste and see that the LORD is good; happy are they who trust in him! Fear the LORD, you that are his saints, for those who fear him lack nothing. The young lions lack and suffer hunger, but those who seek the LORD lack nothing that is good. (Ps. 34:8–10)

Preface: Sundays after Pentecost
Color: Green

*Psalm 80:7–15 (NRSV)
**Psalm 37:1–9 (NRSV)

SUNDAY BETWEEN
OCTOBER 9 AND 15 INCLUSIVE
Proper 23

Prayer of the Day
Almighty God, source of every blessing, your generous goodness comes to us anew every day. By the work of your Spirit lead us to acknowledge your goodness, give thanks for your benefits, and serve you in willing obedience; through your Son, Jesus Christ our Lord. (101)

A
Isaiah 25:1–9
Psalm 23
You spread a table before me, and my cup is running over. (Ps. 23:5)
Philippians 4:1–9
Matthew 22:1–14

B
Amos 5:6–7, 10–15
Psalm 90:12–17
So teach us to number our days that we may apply our hearts to wisdom. (Ps. 90:12)
Hebrews 4:12–16
Mark 10:17–31

C
2 Kings 5:1–3, 7–15c
Psalm 111
I will give thanks to the LORD with my whole heart. (Ps. 111:1)
2 Timothy 2:8–15
Luke 17:11–19

Verse
Alleluia. This is the LORD for whom we have waited; let us be glad and rejoice in his salvation. Alleluia. (Isa. 25:9)

Offertory
If anyone does sin, we have an advocate with the Father, Jesus Christ the righteous; and he is the atoning sacrifice for our sins, and not for ours only but also for the sins of the whole world. See what love the Father has given us, that we should be called children of God: and that is what we are. (1 John 2:1–2; 3:1)

Preface: Sundays after Pentecost
Color: Green

SUNDAY BETWEEN
OCTOBER 16 AND 22 INCLUSIVE
Proper 24

Prayer of the Day
Almighty and everlasting God, in Christ you have revealed your glory among the nations. Preserve the works of your mercy, that your Church throughout the world may persevere with steadfast faith in the confession of your name; through your Son, Jesus Christ our Lord. (102)

A
Isaiah 45:1–7
Psalm 96:1–9 [10–13]
Ascribe to the LORD honor and power.
(Ps. 96:7)
1 Thessalonians 1:1–10
Matthew 22:15–22

B
Isaiah 53:4–12
Psalm 91:9–16
You have made the LORD your refuge, and the Most High your habitation. (Ps. 91:9)
Hebrews 5:1–10
Mark 10:35–45

C
Genesis 32:22–31
Psalm 121
My help comes from the LORD, the maker of heaven and earth. (Ps. 121:2)
2 Timothy 3:14—4:5
Luke 18:1–8

Verse
Alleluia. In fulfillment of his own purpose God gave us birth by the word of truth, so that we would become a kind of first fruits of his creatures. Alleluia. (James 1:18)

Offertory
The cup of blessing that we bless, is it not a sharing in the blood of Christ? The bread that we break, is it not a sharing in the body of Christ? Because there is one bread, we who are many are one body, for we all partake of the one bread. (1 Cor. 10:16–17)

Preface: Sundays after Pentecost
Color: Green

SUNDAY BETWEEN
OCTOBER 23 AND 29 INCLUSIVE
Proper 25

Prayer of the Day
Almighty and everlasting God, increase in us the gifts of faith, hope, and charity; and, that we may obtain what you promise, make us love what you command; through your Son, Jesus Christ our Lord. (103)

A
Leviticus 19:1–2, 15–18
Psalm 1
Their delight is in the law of the LORD. (Ps. 1:2)
1 Thessalonians 2:1–8
Matthew 22:34–46

B
Jeremiah 31:7–9
Psalm 126
Those who sowed with tears will reap with songs of joy. (Ps. 126:6)
Hebrews 7:23–28
Mark 10:46–52

C
Jeremiah 14:7–10, 19–22
(*or* Sirach 35:12–17)
Psalm 84:1–6*
Happy are the people whose strength is in you. (Ps. 84:4)
2 Timothy 4:6–8, 16–18
Luke 18:9–14

Verse
Alleluia. The Lord will rescue me from every evil attack and save me for his heavenly kingdom. Alleluia. (2 Tim. 4:18)

Offertory
Worthy is the Lamb that was slain to receive power and wealth and wisdom and might and honor and glory and blessing! To the one seated on the throne and to the Lamb be blessing and honor and glory and might forever and ever! Amen! (Rev. 5:12–14)

Preface: Sundays after Pentecost
Color: Green

*Psalm 84:1–7 (NRSV)

SUNDAY BETWEEN OCTOBER 30 AND NOVEMBER 5 INCLUSIVE
Proper 26

Prayer of the Day
Stir up, O Lord, the wills of your faithful people to seek more eagerly the help you offer, that, at the last, they may enjoy the fruit of salvation; through our Lord Jesus Christ. (105)

A
Micah 3:5–12
Psalm 43
Send out your light and truth that they may lead me. (Ps. 43:3)
1 Thessalonians 2:9–13
Matthew 23:1–12

B
Deuteronomy 6:1–9
Psalm 119:1–8
Happy are they who seek the LORD with all their hearts. (Ps. 119:2)
Hebrews 9:11–14
Mark 12:28–34

C
Isaiah 1:10–18
Psalm 32:1–8*
All the faithful will make their prayers to you in time of trouble. (Ps. 32:7)
2 Thessalonians 1:1–4, 11–12
Luke 19:1–10

Verse
Alleluia. Let the word of the Lord spread rapidly and be glorified everywhere, for the Lord is faithful and will strengthen you. Alleluia. (2 Thess. 3:1, 3)

Offertory
Hallelujah! For the Lord our God the Almighty reigns. Let us rejoice and exult and give him the glory, for the marriage of the Lamb has come, and his bride has made herself ready. Blessed are those who are invited to the marriage supper of the Lamb. (Rev. 19:6–7, 9)

Preface: Sundays after Pentecost
Color: Green

*Psalm 32:1–7 (NRSV)

SUNDAY BETWEEN NOVEMBER 6 AND 12 INCLUSIVE
Proper 27

Prayer of the Day
Lord, when the day of wrath comes we have no hope except in your grace. Make us so to watch for the last days that the consummation of our hope may be the joy of the marriage feast of your Son, Jesus Christ our Lord. (104)

A
Amos 5:18–24
(*or* Wisdom of Solomon 6:12–16)
Psalm 70 (*or* Wisdom of Solomon 6:17–20)
You are my helper and my deliverer; O LORD, do not tarry. (Ps. 70:6) or *The beginning of wisdom is the most sincere desire for instruction. (Wisdom of Solomon 6:17)*
1 Thessalonians 4:13–18
Matthew 25:1–13

B
1 Kings 17:8–16
Psalm 146
The LORD lifts up those who are bowed down. (Ps. 146:7)
Hebrews 9:24–28
Mark 12:38–44

C
Job 19:23–27a
Psalm 17:1–9
Keep me as the apple of your eye; hide me under the shadow of your wings. (Ps. 17:8)
2 Thessalonians 2:1–5, 13–17
Luke 20:27–38

Verse
Alleluia. Keep awake therefore, for you do not know on what day your Lord is coming. Alleluia. (Matt. 24:42)

Offertory
Hallelujah! For the Lord our God the Almighty reigns. Let us rejoice and exult and give him the glory, for the marriage of the Lamb has come, and his bride has made herself ready. Blessed are those who are invited to the marriage supper of the Lamb. (Rev. 19:6–7, 9)

Preface: Sundays after Pentecost
Color: Green

SUNDAY BETWEEN
NOVEMBER 13 AND 19 INCLUSIVE
Proper 28

Prayer of the Day
Lord God, so rule and govern our hearts
and minds by your Holy Spirit that, always
keeping in mind the end of all things and
the day of judgment, we may be stirred up
to holiness of life here and may live with
you forever in the world to come, through
your Son, Jesus Christ our Lord. (106)

or

Almighty and ever-living God, before the
earth was formed and even after it ceases to
be, you are God. Break into our short span
of life and let us see the signs of your final
will and purpose, through your Son, Jesus
Christ our Lord. (107)

A
Zephaniah 1:7, 12–18
Psalm 90:1–8 [9–11] 12
*So teach us to number our days, that we may
apply our hearts to wisdom. (Ps. 90:12)*
1 Thessalonians 5:1–11
Matthew 25:14–30

B
Daniel 12:1–3
Psalm 16
*My heart is glad and my spirit rejoices; my
body shall rest in hope. (Ps. 16:9)*
Hebrews 10:11–14 [15–18] 19–25
Mark 13:1–8

C
Malachi 4:1–2a
Psalm 98
*In righteousness shall the LORD judge the
world. (Ps. 98:10)*
2 Thessalonians 3:6–13
Luke 21:5–19

Verse
Alleluia. The Lord says, "Surely I am com-
ing soon." Amen. Come, Lord Jesus!
Alleluia. (Rev. 22:20)

Offertory
We give you thanks, Lord God Almighty,
who are and who were, for you have taken
your great power and begun to reign. Fear
God and give him glory, for the hour of his
judgment has come; and worship him who
made heaven and earth, the sea and the
springs of water. (Rev. 11:17; 14:7)

Preface: Sundays after Pentecost
Color: Green

CHRIST THE KING
SUNDAY BETWEEN
NOVEMBER 20 AND 26 INCLUSIVE
Last Sunday after Pentecost
Proper 29

Prayer of the Day
Almighty and everlasting God, whose will it
is to restore all things to your beloved Son,
whom you anointed priest forever and king
of all creation: Grant that all the people of
the earth, now divided by the power of sin,
may be united under the glorious and gentle rule of your Son, our Lord Jesus Christ,
who lives and reigns with you and the Holy
Spirit, one God, now and forever. (108)

A
Ezekiel 34:11–16, 20–24
Psalm 95:1–7a
*We are the people of God's pasture and the
sheep of God's hand. (Ps. 95:7)*
Ephesians 1:15–23
Matthew 25:31–46

B
Daniel 7:9–10, 13–14
Psalm 93
*Ever since the world began, your throne has
been established. (Ps. 93:3)*
Revelation 1:4b–8
John 18:33–37

C
Jeremiah 23:1–6
Psalm 46
I will be exalted among the nations. (Ps. 46:11)
Colossians 1:11–20
Luke 23:33–43

Verse
Alleluia. I am the Alpha and the Omega,
the first and the last, the beginning and the
end. Alleluia. (Rev. 22:13)

Offertory
Beloved, we are God's children now; what
we will be has not yet been revealed. What
we do know is this: when he is revealed we
will be like him, for we will see him as he is.
And all who have this hope in him purify
themselves, just as he is pure. (1 John 3:2–3)

Preface: Sundays after Pentecost *or* Christ
the King
Color: White

LESSER FESTIVALS

ST. ANDREW, APOSTLE
November 30

Prayer of the Day
Almighty God, as the apostle Andrew readily obeyed the call of Christ and followed him without delay, grant that we, called by your holy Word, may in glad obedience offer ourselves to your service; through your Son, Jesus Christ our Lord, who lives and reigns with you and the Holy Spirit, one God, now and forever. (109)

A, B, C
Ezekiel 3:16–21
Psalm 19:1–6
Their sound has gone out into all lands.
(Ps. 19:4)
Romans 10:10–18
John 1:35–42

Verse
Alleluia. You will be my witnesses in Jerusalem, in all Judea and Samaria, and to the ends of the earth. Alleluia. (Acts 1:8)

Offertory
Sing to the LORD and bless his name; proclaim the good news of his salvation from day to day. Declare his glory among the nations and his wonders among all peoples. For great is the LORD and greatly to be praised. Oh, the majesty and magnificence of his presence! Oh, the power and the splendor of his sanctuary! (Ps. 96:2–4, 6)

Preface: Apostles
Color: Red

ST. THOMAS, APOSTLE
December 21

Prayer of the Day
Almighty and ever-living God, you have given great and precious promises to those who believe. Grant us that perfect faith which overcomes all doubts; through your Son, Jesus Christ our Lord, who lives and reigns with you and the Holy Spirit, one God, now and forever. (110)

A, B, C
Judges 6:36–40
Psalm 136:1–4, 23–26
God's mercy endures forever. (Ps. 136:1b)
Ephesians 4:11–16
John 14:1–7

Verse
Alleluia. You will be my witnesses in Jerusalem, in all Judea and Samaria, and to the ends of the earth. Alleluia. (Acts 1:8)

Offertory
Sing to the LORD and bless his name; proclaim the good news of his salvation from day to day. Declare his glory among the nations and his wonders among all peoples. For great is the LORD and greatly to be praised. Oh, the majesty and magnificence of his presence! Oh, the power and the splendor of his sanctuary! (Ps. 96:2–4, 6)

Preface: Apostles
Color: Red

ST. STEPHEN, DEACON AND MARTYR
December 26

Prayer of the Day
Grant us grace, O Lord, that like Stephen we may learn to love even our enemies and seek forgiveness for those who desire our hurt; through your Son, Jesus Christ our Lord, who lives and reigns with you and the Holy Spirit, one God, now and forever. (111)

A, B, C
2 Chronicles 24:17–22
Psalm 17:1–9, 16*
I call upon you, O God, for you will answer me. (Ps. 17:6)
Acts 6:8—7:2a, 51–60
Matthew 23:34–39

Verse
Alleluia. Blessed are those who are persecuted for righteousness' sake, for theirs is the kingdom of heaven. Alleluia. (Matt. 5:10)

Offertory
I put my trust in the LORD. I will rejoice and be glad because of your mercy. Make your face to shine upon your servant, and in your lovingkindness save me. You hide in the covert of your presence those who trust in you; you keep them in your shelter from the strife of tongues. (Ps. 31:6–7, 16, 20)

Preface: Christmas
Color: Red

*Psalm 17:1–9, 15 (NRSV̂)

ST. JOHN, APOSTLE AND EVANGELIST
December 27

Prayer of the Day
Merciful Lord, let the brightness of your light shine on your Church, so that all of us, instructed by the teachings of John, your apostle and evangelist, may walk in the light of your truth and attain eternal life; through your Son, Jesus Christ our Lord, who lives and reigns with you and the Holy Spirit, one God, now and forever. (112)

A, B, C
Genesis 1:1–5, 26–31
Psalm 116:10–17*
Precious in your sight, O LORD, is the death of your servants. (Ps. 116:13)
1 John 1:1—2:2
John 21:20–25

Verse
Alleluia. For the message about the cross is the power of God to us who are being saved. Alleluia. (1 Cor. 1:18)

Offertory
The gifts Christ gave were that some would be apostles, some prophets, some evangelists, some pastors and teachers, to equip the saints for the work of ministry, for building up the body of Christ, until all of us come to the unity of the faith and of the knowledge of the Son of God. (Eph. 4:11–13)

Preface: Apostles *or* Christmas
Color: White

**Psalm 116:12–19 (NRSV)*

THE HOLY INNOCENTS, MARTYRS
December 28

Prayer of the Day
We remember today, O God, the slaughter of the holy innocents of Bethlehem by order of King Herod. Receive, we pray, into the arms of your mercy all innocent victims, and by your great might frustrate the designs of evil tyrants and establish your rule of justice, love, and peace; through Jesus Christ our Lord, who lives and reigns with you and the Holy Spirit, one God, now and forever. (113)

A, B, C
Jeremiah 31:15–17
Psalm 124
We have escaped like a bird from the snare of the fowler. (Ps. 124:7)
1 Peter 4:12–19
Matthew 2:13–18

Verse
Alleluia. Blessed are those who are persecuted for righteousness' sake, for theirs is the kingdom of heaven. Alleluia. (Matt. 5:10)

Offertory
I put my trust in the LORD. I will rejoice and be glad because of your mercy. Make your face to shine upon your servant, and in your lovingkindness save me. You hide in the covert of your presence those who trust in you; you keep them in your shelter from the strife of tongues. (Ps. 31:6–7, 16, 20)

Preface: Christmas
Color: Red

THE NAME OF JESUS
January 1

Prayer of the Day
Eternal Father, you gave your Son the name of Jesus to be a sign of our salvation. Plant in every heart the love of the Savior of the world, Jesus Christ our Lord, who lives and reigns with you and the Holy Spirit, one God, now and forever. (114)

A, B, C
Numbers 6:22–27
Psalm 8
How exalted is your name in all the world. (Ps. 8:1)
Galatians 4:4–7 *or* Philippians 2:5–11
Luke 2:15–21

Verse
Alleluia. At the name of Jesus every knee should bend, in heaven and on earth and under the earth. Alleluia. (Phil. 2:10)

Offertory
Offer to God a sacrifice of thanksgiving, and make good your vows to the Most High. Whoever offers me the sacrifice of thanksgiving honors me; but to those who keep in my way will I show the salvation of God. (Ps. 50:14, 23)

Preface: Christmas
Color: White

THE CONFESSION OF ST. PETER
January 18

Prayer of the Day

Almighty God, you inspired Simon Peter to confess Jesus as the Messiah and Son of the living God. Keep your Church firm on the rock of this faith, that in unity and peace it may proclaim one truth and follow one Lord, your Son, our Savior Jesus Christ, who lives and reigns with you and the Holy Spirit, one God, now and forever. (115)

A, B, C

Acts 4:8–13
Psalm 18:1–7, 17–20*
My God, my rock, you are worthy of praise.
(Ps. 18:2)
1 Corinthians 10:1–5
Matthew 16:13–19

Verse

Alleluia. You will be my witnesses in Jerusalem, in all Judea and Samaria, and to the ends of the earth. Alleluia. (Acts 1:8)

Offertory

Sing to the LORD and bless his name; proclaim the good news of his salvation from day to day. Declare his glory among the nations and his wonders among all peoples. For great is the LORD and greatly to be praised. Oh, the majesty and magnificence of his presence! Oh, the power and the splendor of his sanctuary! (Ps. 96:2–4, 6)

Preface: Apostles
Color: White

*Psalm 18:1–6, 16–19 (NRSV)

THE CONVERSION OF ST. PAUL
January 25

Prayer of the Day

Lord God, through the preaching of your apostle Paul, you established one Church from among the nations. As we celebrate his conversion, we pray that we may follow his example and be witnesses to the truth in your Son, Jesus Christ our Lord, who lives and reigns with you and the Holy Spirit, one God, now and forever. (116)

A, B, C

Acts 9:1–22
Psalm 67
Let all the peoples praise you, O God. (Ps. 67:3)
Galatians 1:11–24
Luke 21:10–19

Verse

Alleluia. This Jesus God raised up, and of that all of us are witnesses. Alleluia. (Acts 2:32)

Offertory

Sing to the LORD and bless his name; proclaim the good news of his salvation from day to day. Declare his glory among the nations and his wonders among all peoples. For great is the LORD and greatly to be praised. Oh, the majesty and magnificence of his presence! Oh, the power and the splendor of his sanctuary! (Ps. 96:2–4, 6)

Preface: Apostles
Color: White

THE PRESENTATION OF OUR LORD
February 2

Prayer of the Day

Blessed are you, O Lord our God, for you have sent us your salvation. Inspire us by your Holy Spirit to see with our own eyes him who is the glory of Israel and the light for all nations, your Son, Jesus Christ our Lord. (117)

A, B, C

Malachi 3:1–4
Psalm 84 *or* Psalm 24:7–10
How dear to me is your dwelling, O LORD.
(Ps. 84:1) or *Lift up your heads, O gates, and the King of glory shall come in. (Ps. 24:7)*
Hebrews 2:14–18
Luke 2:22–40

Verse

Alleluia. My eyes have seen your salvation. Alleluia. (Luke 2:30)

Offertory

Offer to God a sacrifice of thanksgiving, and make good your vows to the Most High. Whoever offers me the sacrifice of thanksgiving honors me; but to those who keep in my way will I show the salvation of God. (Ps. 50:14, 23)

Preface: Christmas
Color: White

ST. MATTHIAS, APOSTLE
February 24

Prayer of the Day
Almighty God, you chose your faithful servant Matthias to be numbered among the Twelve. Grant that your Church, being delivered from false apostles, may always be taught and guided by faithful and true pastors; through your Son, Jesus Christ our Lord, who lives and reigns with you and the Holy Spirit, one God, now and forever. (118)

A, B, C
Isaiah 66:1–2
Psalm 56
I am bound by the vow I made to you, O God. (Ps. 56:11)
Acts 1:15–26
Luke 6:12–16

Verse
Alleluia. Whoever serves me, the Father will honor. Alleluia. (John 12:26)

Offertory
Lord, you guide me along right pathways for your name's sake. You spread a table before me in the presence of those who trouble me; you have anointed my head with oil, and my cup is running over. Surely your goodness and mercy shall follow me all the days of my life, and I will dwell in the house of the Lord forever. (Ps. 23:3–6)

Preface: Apostles
Color: Red

THE ANNUNCIATION OF OUR LORD
March 25

Prayer of the Day
Pour your grace into our hearts, O Lord, that we, who have known the incarnation of your Son, Jesus Christ, announced by an angel, may by his cross and Passion be brought to the glory of his resurrection; who lives and reigns with you and the Holy Spirit, one God, now and forever. (119)

A, B, C
Isaiah 7:10–14
Psalm 45 *or* Psalm 40:5–11*
I will make your name to be remembered from one generation to another. (Ps. 45:18)
or *I love to do your will, O my God. (Ps. 40:9)*
Hebrews 10:4–10
Luke 1:26–38

Verse
Alleluia. Greetings, O favored one! The Lord is with you. The Holy Spirit will come upon you. Alleluia. (Luke 1:28, 35) *or* Alleluia. From this day all generations will call me blessed: the Almighty has done great things for me, and holy is his name. Alleluia. (Luke 1:48–49)

Offertory
Who is like the Lord our God, who sits enthroned on high, but stoops to behold the heavens and the earth? He takes up the weak out of the dust, and lifts up the poor from the ashes. He sets them with the princes, with the princes of his people. (Ps. 113:5–8)

Preface: Christmas
Color: White

*Psalm 40:5–10 (NRSV)

ST. MARK, EVANGELIST
April 25

Prayer of the Day
Almighty God, you have enriched your Church with Mark's proclamation of the Gospel. Give us grace to believe firmly in the good news of salvation and to walk daily in accord with it; through your Son, Jesus Christ our Lord, who lives and reigns with you and the Holy Spirit, one God, now and forever. (120)

A, B, C
Isaiah 52:7–10
Psalm 57
I will confess you among the peoples, O Lord. (Ps. 57:9)
2 Timothy 4:6–11, 18
Mark 1:1–15

Verse
Alleluia. This Jesus God raised up, and of that all of us are witnesses. Alleluia. (Acts 2:32)

Offertory
Sing to the Lord and bless his name; proclaim the good news of his salvation from day to day. Declare his glory among the nations and his wonders among all peoples. For great is the Lord and greatly to be praised. Oh, the majesty and magnificence of his presence! Oh, the power and the splendor of his sanctuary! (Ps. 96:2–4, 6)

Preface: All Saints
Color: Red

ST. PHILIP AND ST. JAMES, APOSTLES
May 1

Prayer of the Day
Almighty God, to know you is to have eternal life. Grant us to know your Son as the way, the truth, and the life; and guide our footsteps along the way of Jesus Christ our Lord, who lives and reigns with you and the Holy Spirit, one God, now and forever. (121)

A, B, C
Isaiah 30:18–21
Psalm 44:1–3, 20–26
Save us for the sake of your steadfast love.
(Ps. 44:26)
2 Corinthians 4:1–6
John 14:8–14

Verse
Alleluia. You will be my witnesses in Jerusalem, in all Judea and Samaria, and to the ends of the earth. Alleluia. (Acts 1:8)

Offertory
Sing to the LORD and bless his name; proclaim the good news of his salvation from day to day. Declare his glory among the nations and his wonders among all peoples. For great is the LORD and greatly to be praised. Oh, the majesty and magnificence of his presence! Oh, the power and the splendor of his sanctuary! (Ps. 96:2–4, 6)

Preface: Apostles
Color: Red

THE VISITATION
May 31

Prayer of the Day
Almighty God, in choosing the virgin Mary to be the mother of your Son, you made known your gracious regard for the poor and the lowly and the despised. Grant us grace to receive your Word in humility, and so to be made one with your Son, Jesus Christ our Lord, who lives and reigns with you and the Holy Spirit, one God, now and forever. (122)

A, B, C
1 Samuel 2:1–10
Psalm 113
Let the name of the LORD be blessed from this time forth forevermore. (Ps. 113:2)
Romans 12:9–16b
Luke 1:39–57

Verse
Alleluia. My eyes have seen your salvation. Alleluia. (Luke 2:30)

Offertory
Offer to God a sacrifice of thanksgiving, and make good your vows to the Most High. Whoever offers me the sacrifice of thanksgiving honors me; but to those who keep in my way will I show the salvation of God. (Ps. 50:14, 23)

Preface: Christmas
Color: White

ST. BARNABAS, APOSTLE
June 11

Prayer of the Day
Grant, almighty God, that we may follow the example of your faithful servant Barnabas, who, seeking not his own renown but the well-being of your Church, gave generously of his life and substance for the relief of the poor and the spread of the Gospel; through Jesus Christ our Lord, who lives and reigns with you and the Holy Spirit, one God, now and forever. (123)

A, B, C
Isaiah 42:5–12
Psalm 112
Happy are they who fear the LORD. (Ps. 112:1)
Acts 11:19–30; 13:1–3
Matthew 10:7–16

Verse
Alleluia. This Jesus God raised up, and of that all of us are witnesses. Alleluia. (Acts 2:32)

Offertory
Sing to the LORD and bless his name; proclaim the good news of his salvation from day to day. Declare his glory among the nations and his wonders among all peoples. For great is the LORD and greatly to be praised. Oh, the majesty and magnificence of his presence! Oh, the power and the splendor of his sanctuary! (Ps. 96:2–4, 6)

Preface: Apostles
Color: Red

THE NATIVITY OF ST. JOHN THE BAPTIST
June 24

Prayer of the Day
Almighty God, you called John the Baptist to give witness to the coming of your Son and to prepare his way. Grant to your people the wisdom to see your purpose and the openness to hear your will, that we too may witness to Christ's coming and so prepare his way; through your Son, Jesus Christ our Lord, who lives and reigns with you and the Holy Spirit, one God, now and forever. (124)

A, B, C
Malachi 3:1–4
Psalm 141
My eyes are turned to you, Lord GOD.
(Ps. 141:8)
Acts 13:13–26
Luke 1:57–67 [68–80]

Verse
Alleluia. Blessed are those who are persecuted for righteousness' sake, for theirs is the kingdom of heaven. Alleluia. (Matt. 5:10)

Offertory
I put my trust in the LORD. I will rejoice and be glad because of your mercy. Make your face to shine upon your servant, and in your lovingkindness save me. You hide in the covert of your presence those who trust in you; you keep them in your shelter from the strife of tongues. (Ps. 31:6–7, 16, 20)

Preface: Advent
Color: White

ST. PETER AND ST. PAUL, APOSTLES
June 29

Prayer of the Day
Almighty God, whose blessed apostles Peter and Paul glorified you by their martyrdom: Grant that your Church, instructed by their teaching and example, and knit together in unity by your Spirit, may ever stand firm upon the one foundation, which is Jesus Christ our Lord, who lives and reigns with you and the Holy Spirit, one God, now and forever. (125)

A, B, C
Ezekiel 34:11–16
Psalm 87:1–2, 4–6*
Glorious things are spoken of you, O city of our God. (Ps. 87:2)

1 Corinthians 3:16–23
Mark 8:27–35

Verse
Alleluia. This Jesus God raised up, and of that all of us are witnesses. Alleluia. (Acts 2:32)

Offertory
Sing to the LORD and bless his name; proclaim the good news of his salvation from day to day. Declare his glory among the nations and his wonders among all peoples. For great is the LORD and greatly to be praised. Oh, the majesty and magnificence of his presence! Oh, the power and the splendor of his sanctuary! (Ps. 96:2–4, 6)

Preface: Apostles
Color: Red

Psalm 87:1–3, 5–7 (NRSV)

ST. MARY MAGDALENE
July 22

Prayer of the Day
Almighty God, your Son Jesus Christ restored Mary Magdalene to health of body and mind, and called her to be a witness of his resurrection. Heal us now in body and mind, and call us to serve you in the power of the resurrection of Jesus Christ, who lives and reigns with you and the Holy Spirit, one God, now and forever. (126)

A, B, C
Ruth 1:6–18 *or* Exodus 2:1–10
Psalm 73:23–29*
I will speak of all your works in the gates of the city of Zion. (Ps. 73:29)
Acts 13:26–33a
John 20:1–2, 11–18

Verse
Alleluia. Whoever serves me, the Father will honor. Alleluia. (John 12:26)

Offertory
LORD, you guide me along right pathways for your name's sake. You spread a table before me in the presence of those who trouble me; you have anointed my head with oil, and my cup is running over. Surely your goodness and mercy shall follow me all the days of my life, and I will dwell in the house of the LORD forever. (Ps. 23:3–6)

Preface: All Saints
Color: White

Psalm 73:23–28 (NRSV)

ST. JAMES THE ELDER, APOSTLE
July 25

Prayer of the Day
O gracious God, we remember before you today your servant and apostle James, first among the Twelve to suffer martyrdom for the name of Jesus Christ. Pour out upon the leaders of your Church that spirit of self-denying service which is the true mark of authority among your people; through Jesus Christ our Lord, who lives and reigns with you and the Holy Spirit, one God, now and forever. (127)

A, B, C
1 Kings 19:9–18
Psalm 7:1–11*
God is my shield and defense. (Ps. 7:11)
Acts 11:27—12:3a
Mark 10:35–45

Verse
Alleluia. Blessed are those who are persecuted for righteousness' sake, for theirs is the kingdom of heaven. Alleluia. (Matt. 5:10)

Offertory
I put my trust in the LORD. I will rejoice and be glad because of your mercy. Make your face to shine upon your servant, and in your lovingkindness save me. You hide in the covert of your presence those who trust in you; you keep them in your shelter from the strife of tongues. (Ps. 31:6–7, 16, 20)

Preface: Apostles
Color: Red

Psalm 7:1–10 (NRSV)

MARY, MOTHER OF OUR LORD
August 15

Prayer of the Day
Almighty God, you chose the virgin Mary to be the mother of your only Son. Grant that we, who have been redeemed by his blood, may share with her in the glory of your eternal kingdom; through your Son, Jesus Christ our Lord, who lives and reigns with you and the Holy Spirit, one God, now and forever. (128)

A, B, C
Isaiah 61:7–11
Psalm 45:11–16*
I will make your name to be remembered from one generation to another. (Ps. 45:18)

Galatians 4:4–7
Luke 1:46–55

Verse
Alleluia. Greetings, O favored one! The Lord is with you. The Holy Spirit will come upon you. Alleluia. (Luke 1:28, 35) *or* Alleluia. From this day all generations will call me blessed: the Almighty has done great things for me, and holy is his name. Alleluia. (Luke 1:48–49)

Offertory
Who is like the LORD our God, who sits enthroned on high, but stoops to behold the heavens and the earth? He takes up the weak out of the dust, and lifts up the poor from the ashes. He sets them with the princes, with the princes of his people. (Ps. 113:5–8)

Preface: All Saints
Color: White

Psalm 45:10–15 (NRSV)

ST. BARTHOLOMEW, APOSTLE
August 24

Prayer of the Day
Almighty and everlasting God, who gave to your apostle Bartholomew grace truly to believe and to preach your Word: Grant that your Church may love what he believed and preach what he taught; through your Son, Jesus Christ our Lord, who lives and reigns with you and the Holy Spirit, one God, now and forever. (129)

A, B, C
Exodus 19:1–6
Psalm 12
The words of the LORD are pure. (Ps. 12:6)
1 Corinthians 12:27–31a
John 1:43–51

Verse
Alleluia. How beautiful upon the mountains are the feet of the messenger who announces peace, who brings good news, who announces salvation. Alleluia. (Isa. 52:7)

Offertory
Sing to the LORD and bless his name; proclaim the good news of his salvation from day to day. Declare his glory among the nations and his wonders among all peoples.

For great is the Lord and greatly to be praised. Oh, the majesty and magnificence of his presence! Oh, the power and the splendor of his sanctuary! (Ps. 96:2–4, 6)

Preface: Apostles
Color: Red

HOLY CROSS DAY
September 14

Prayer of the Day
Almighty God, your Son Jesus Christ was lifted high upon the cross so that he might draw the whole world to himself. Grant that we who glory in his death for our salvation may also glory in his call to take up our cross and follow him; through your Son, Jesus Christ our Lord, who lives and reigns with you and the Holy Spirit, one God, now and forever. (130)

A, B, C
Numbers 21:4b–9
Psalm 98:1–5* *or* Psalm 78:1–2, 34–38
The Lord has done marvelous things. (Ps. 98:1) or *God was their rock and the Most High God their redeemer. (Ps. 78:35)*
1 Corinthians 1:18–24
John 3:13–17

Verse
Alleluia. May I never boast of anything except the cross of our Lord Jesus Christ. Alleluia. (Gal. 6:14)

Offertory
Christ Jesus emptied himself and became obedient to the point of death—even death on a cross. Therefore God also highly exalted him and gave him the name that is above every name, so that at the name of Jesus every knee should bend, and every tongue should confess that Jesus Christ is Lord, to the glory of God the Father. (Phil. 2:7–11)

Preface: Passion
Color: Red

*Psalm 98:1–4 (NRSV)

ST. MATTHEW, APOSTLE AND EVANGELIST
September 21

Prayer of the Day
Almighty God, your Son our Savior called a despised collector of taxes to become one of his apostles. Help us, like Matthew, to respond to the transforming call of your Son, Jesus Christ our Lord, who lives and reigns with you and the Holy Spirit, one God, now and forever. (131)

A, B, C
Ezekiel 2:8—3:11
Psalm 119:33–40
Teach me, O Lord, the way of your statutes. (Ps. 119:33)
Ephesians 2:4–10
Matthew 9:9–13

Verse
Alleluia. You will be my witnesses in Jerusalem, in all Judea and Samaria, and to the ends of the earth. Alleluia. (Acts 1:8)

Offertory
Sing to the Lord and bless his name; proclaim the good news of his salvation from day to day. Declare his glory among the nations and his wonders among all peoples. For great is the Lord and greatly to be praised. Oh, the majesty and magnificence of his presence! Oh, the power and the splendor of his sanctuary! (Ps. 96:2–4, 6)

Preface: Apostles
Color: Red

ST. MICHAEL AND ALL ANGELS
September 29

Prayer of the Day
Everlasting God, you have ordained and constituted in a wonderful order the ministries of angels and mortals. Mercifully grant that, as your holy angels always serve and worship you in heaven, so by your appointment they may help and defend us here on earth; through your Son, Jesus Christ our Lord, who lives and reigns with you and the Holy Spirit, one God, now and forever. (132)

A, B, C
Daniel 10:10–14; 12:1–3
Psalm 103:1–5, 20–22
Bless the LORD, you angels of the LORD.
(Ps. 103:20)
Revelation 12:7–12
Luke 10:17–20

Verse
Alleluia. Bless the LORD, you angels of the
LORD, you mighty ones who do his bidding.
Alleluia. (Ps. 103:20)

Offertory
Then I looked, and I heard the voice of
many angels surrounding the throne and
the living creatures and the elders; they
numbered myriads of myriads and thousands of thousands, singing with full voice,
"Worthy is the Lamb that was slain to
receive power and wealth and wisdom and
might and honor and glory and blessing!"
(Rev. 5:11–12)

Preface: Weekdays *or* Sundays after
Pentecost
Color: White

ST. LUKE, EVANGELIST
October 18

Prayer of the Day
Almighty God, you inspired your servant
Luke the physician to reveal in his Gospel
the love and healing power of your Son.
Give your Church the same love and power
to heal, to the glory of your name; through
your Son, Jesus Christ our Lord, who lives
and reigns with you and the Holy Spirit, one
God, now and forever. (133)

A, B, C
Isaiah 43:8–13 *or* Isaiah 35:5–8
Psalm 124
Our help is in the name of the LORD.
(Ps. 124:8)
2 Timothy 4:5–11
Luke 1:1–4; 24:44–53

Verse
Alleluia. How beautiful upon the mountains
are the feet of the messenger who announces
peace, who brings good news, who
announces salvation. Alleluia. (Isa. 52:7)

Offertory
Sing to the LORD and bless his name; proclaim the good news of his salvation from
day to day. Declare his glory among the
nations and his wonders among all peoples.
For great is the LORD and greatly to be
praised. Oh, the majesty and magnificence
of his presence! Oh, the power and the
splendor of his sanctuary! (Ps. 96:2–4, 6)

Preface: All Saints
Color: Red

ST. SIMON AND ST. JUDE, APOSTLES
October 28

Prayer of the Day
O God, we thank you for the glorious company of the apostles and, especially on this
day, for Simon and Jude. We pray that, as
they were faithful and zealous in their mission, so we may with ardent devotion make
known the love and mercy of our Lord and
Savior Jesus Christ, who lives and reigns
with you and the Holy Spirit, one God,
now and forever. (134)

A, B, C
Jeremiah 26:[1–6] 7–16
Psalm 11
In the LORD have I taken refuge. (Ps. 11:1)
1 John 4:1–6
John 14:21–27

Verse
Alleluia. You will be my witnesses in
Jerusalem, in all Judea and Samaria, and to
the ends of the earth. Alleluia. (Acts 1:8)

Offertory
Sing to the LORD and bless his name; proclaim the good news of his salvation from
day to day. Declare his glory among the
nations and his wonders among all peoples.
For great is the LORD and greatly to be
praised. Oh, the majesty and magnificence
of his presence! Oh, the power and the
splendor of his sanctuary! (Ps. 96:2–4, 6)

Preface: Apostles
Color: Red

REFORMATION DAY
October 31

Prayer of the Day
Almighty God, gracious Lord, pour out
your Holy Spirit upon your faithful people.
Keep them steadfast in your Word, protect
and comfort them in all temptations, defend
them against all their enemies, and bestow
on the Church your saving peace; through
your Son, Jesus Christ our Lord, who lives
and reigns with you and the Holy Spirit, one
God, now and forever. (135)

A, B, C
Jeremiah 31:31–34
Psalm 46
*The LORD of hosts is with us; the God of
Jacob is our stronghold. (Ps. 46:4)*
Romans 3:19–28
John 8:31–36

Verse
Alleluia. If you continue in my word, you
are truly my disciples, and you will know
the truth, and the truth will make you free.
Alleluia. (John 8:31–32)

Offertory
I appeal to you, therefore, by the mercies
of God, to present your bodies as a living
sacrifice, holy and acceptable to God,
which is your spiritual worship. Do not
be conformed to this world, but be transformed by the renewing of your minds,
so that you may discern what is the will of
God—what is good and acceptable and
perfect. (Rom. 12:1–2)

Preface: Weekdays *or* Sundays after
Pentecost
Color: Red

A
Revelation 7:9–17
Psalm 34:1–10, 22
Fear the LORD, you saints of the LORD.
(Ps. 34:9)
1 John 3:1–3
Matthew 5:1–12

B
Isaiah 25:6–9
(*or* Wisdom of Solomon 3:1–9)
Psalm 24
*They shall receive a blessing from the God
of their salvation. (Ps. 24:5)*
Revelation 21:1–6a
John 11:32–44

C
Daniel 7:1–3, 15–18
Psalm 149
*Sing the praise of the LORD in the congrega-
tion of the faithful. (Ps. 149:1)*
Ephesians 1:11–23
Luke 6:20–31

Verse
Alleluia. They are before the throne of
God, and the one seated on the throne will
shelter them. Alleluia. (Rev. 7:15)

Offertory
Let us rejoice and exult and give God the
glory, for the marriage of the Lamb has
come, and his Bride has made herself ready;
to her it has been granted to be clothed
with fine linen, bright and pure—for the
fine linen is the righteous deeds of the
saints. (Rev. 19:7–8)

Preface: All Saints
Color: White

ALL SAINTS DAY
November 1

Prayer of the Day
Almighty God, whose people are knit
together in one holy Church, the body of
Christ our Lord: Grant us grace to follow
your blessed saints in lives of faith and
commitment, and to know the inexpressible
joys you have prepared for those who love
you; through your Son, Jesus Christ our
Lord, who lives and reigns with you and the
Holy Spirit, one God, now and forever. (136)

NEW YEAR'S EVE
December 31

Prayer of the Day
Eternal Father, you have placed us in a
world of space and time, and through the
events of our lives you bless us with your
love. Grant that in this new year we may
know your presence, see your love at work,
and live in the light of the event which gives
us joy forever—the coming of your Son,
Jesus Christ our Lord. (159)

A, B, C

Ecclesiastes 3:1–13
Psalm 8
How exalted is your name in all the world.
(Ps. 8:1)
Revelation 21:1–6a
Matthew 25:31–46

Verse
Alleluia. Your word is a lantern to my feet and
a light upon my path. Alleluia. (Ps. 119:105)

Offertory
Be careful then how you live, not as unwise
people but as wise. Be filled with the Spirit,
addressing one another in psalms and hymns
and spiritual songs, singing and making
melody to the Lord with all your heart, always
and for everything giving thanks in the name
of our Lord Jesus Christ to God the Father.
(Eph. 5:15, 18–20)

Preface: Christmas
Color: White

DAY OF THANKSGIVING

Prayer of the Day
Almighty God our Father, your generous
goodness comes to us new every day. By the
work of your Spirit lead us to acknowledge
your goodness, give thanks for your benefits,
and serve you in willing obedience; through
your Son, Jesus Christ our Lord. (155)

A
Deuteronomy 8:7–18
Psalm 65
You crown the year with your goodness, and
your paths overflow with plenty. (Ps. 65:12)
2 Corinthians 9:6–15
Luke 17:11–19

B
Joel 2:21–27
Psalm 126
The LORD has done great things for us, and
we are glad indeed. (Ps. 126:4)
1 Timothy 2:1–7
Matthew 6:25–33

C
Deuteronomy 26:1–11
Psalm 100
Enter the gates of the LORD with thanksgiving.
(Ps. 100:3)
Philippians 4:4–9
John 6:25–35

Verse
Alleluia. God is able to provide you with
every blessing in abundance, so that by
always having enough of everything, you
may share abundantly in every good work.
Alleluia. (2 Cor. 9:8)

Offertory
Mountains and hills, fruit trees and all cedars;
wild beasts and all cattle, creeping things and
winged birds; kings of the earth and all peoples, princes and all rulers of the world; young
men and maidens, old and young together: let
them praise the name of the LORD, for his
name only is exalted, his splendor is over
earth and heaven. (Ps. 148:9–13)

Preface: Weekdays
Color: White

NOTES ON THE PROPERS

The propers contained in this volume are a
harmonization of the the calendar and
propers of *Lutheran Book of Worship*
(1978) with the three-year cycle of readings
appointed in the *Revised Common
Lectionary* (Consultation on Common
Texts, 1992). The Calendar, Prayers of the
Day, Verses, Offertories, Prefaces, and
Colors are taken from *Lutheran Book of
Worship: Ministers Edition*; readings for
Sundays and Principal Festivals as well as
selected Lesser Festivals and
Commemorations are taken from the
Revised Common Lectionary. During the
Sundays after Pentecost, the First Readings
are related to the appointed Gospel, one of
two options offered by the CCT. For Lesser
Festivals and Commemorations which are
not included in the *Revised Common
Lectionary,* readings have been assigned
from *Lutheran Book of Worship.*

Scripture references are based upon the
translation and versification of the *New
Revised Standard Version of the Bible*
(1989) except for the Psalms and Psalm
antiphons which reflect the Psalter of the
Proposed Book of Common Prayer (1976)
as it was emended for use in *Lutheran Book
of Worship.* Since Psalm antiphons were not
included in the *Revised Common
Lectionary,* a new set was developed for use
in this volume.

NOTES ON THE LITURGY

> The following notes describe various ways to use the services of *With One Voice*. These services are based largely on the liturgical material in *Lutheran Book of Worship*. For a complete set of notes on the liturgy, see *Lutheran Book of Worship: Ministers Edition*, pp. 13-39.

> Each service consists of central elements, which are integral to the rite, and supportive elements, which further develop and reveal the essential shape of Christian worship. Supportive elements are often indicated by may; at other places, a variety of suggestions is offered to indicate the flexibility with which each service may be prepared. A description of central and supportive elements in the service of Holy Communion is on pp. 8-9 ("Shape of the Rite").

> Any portion of the service which is set to music may be spoken rather than sung. To be consistent, dialogs between a minister/leader and the congregation, such as ℙ **The Lord be with you** 𝗖 **And also with you**, should be either entirely sung or entirely spoken. Similarly, in *With One Voice* dialogs closely related to spoken portions of the service are not set to music, but are intended to be spoken (such as the salutation preceding the Prayer of the Day).

> Symbols are used to designate the participants in the services. Service portions that are to be led by ordained pastors are marked ℙ (presiding minister). Portions for which leadership by lay persons is preferred are marked 𝗔 (assisting minister). Portions that may be led either by a lay person or a pastor are marked 𝗟 (leader). Portions for the entire congregation are marked 𝗖. In musical portions, those sections marked 𝗜 and 𝗜𝗜 may be sung by alternating groups within the congregation (e.g., men and women, choir and congregation).

> A vertical red line placed between columns indicates a choice of material for that service element. When the options could not be placed in columns, an OR stands between the choices available.

> The numbering and layout of pages in the pew and leaders editions of *With One Voice* are consistent. Seasonal prefaces in the services of Holy Communion are added on pages 22A-D and 36A-D. At the conclusion of "Holy, holy, holy Lord" the page numbering of the pew edition resumes. In both editions, portions assigned to ministers/leaders are in regular type and the congregational portions are in boldface type.

Holy Communion

> The services of Holy Communion in *With One Voice* are numbered consecutively with the three settings in *Lutheran Book of Worship*.

> Only a limited number of alternative texts for leadership portions are provided in the body of these services. Additional texts for the absolution in the Brief Order for Confession and Forgiveness, the greeting, the offertory prayer, the post-communion prayer, and the blessing are provided in *Lutheran Book of Worship* and in *Sundays and Seasons*.

> Eucharistic prayers in the body of the services are selected from those prepared for *Lutheran Book of Worship* and *Occasional Services*. A separate section of eucharistic prayers begins on p. 57. Prayers I-IV are

from the *LBW Ministers Edition*. Prayer V was prepared for Worship '93 (published by the ELCA Division for Congregational Ministries). Prayers A-I, a set of seasonal eucharistic prayers, have been prepared for this volume and are presented for trial use.

> Setting 4 (*Light of Christ*) includes musical choices at the Hymn of Praise and Post-Communion Canticle, as well as an optional musical setting for the Dialogue and Preface in the Great Thanksgiving. Setting 5 (*Bread of Life*) contains a minimum of options in the body of the service and a spoken Great Thanksgiving.

> Setting 6 (*All Times and Places*) is an outline for Holy Communion that enables great flexibility in choosing the elements of the liturgy while ensuring the basic integrity of the rite. It requires careful preparation by worship leaders. Within the fourfold structure (gathering, word, meal, sending), a number of musical settings for the sung portions of the liturgy are offered. These suggestions are by no means an exhaustive list. Brief spoken responses of the congregation are provided in the rite; texts spoken by the ministers may be located in the other Holy Communion settings of this book and of *Lutheran Book of Worship*.

Service of Word and Prayer

> The Service of Word and Prayer may be used at any time a full liturgical order is desired which does not include the Lord's Supper. When used on Sunday, prayers, psalms and readings appointed for the day are appropriate. At other times a daily lectionary may be consulted.

> An ordained minister is not required for the leadership of this service. When the service is led by a lay person, portions marked 𝗟 are intended to be used. When led by an ordained minister, portions marked 𝗟 and ℙ are intended to be used.

> The Service of Word and Prayer offers great flexibility. At several points options for the three cycles of the year (Advent/Christmas, Lent/Easter, Season after Pentecost) are offered. Other appropriate biblical dialogs, scripture songs, Gospel acclamations, offertory songs, offertory prayers, and blessings may be substituted for those presented here.

> The first part of the service centers about the Bible which has been placed on the reading desk. On Sundays, the Holy Gospel and one or two of the other appointed readings are read. At other times, two readings are normally included, one from the Old Testament and one from the New Testament. When a reading from the Gospels is not included, the congregation may remain seated for the readings and the Gospel Acclamation may be omitted.

> The Response to the Word, with its emphasis on renewal of Holy Baptism, may appropriately be led from the font. Other suitable forms of confession and forgiveness may be used. The greeting of peace is included as a sign of reconciliation in Christ.

> When an offering is not received, the service following the Peace may be concluded with the Prayers, Lord's Prayer, Blessing, Sending Song and Dismissal.

Acknowledgments

The liturgical material on pages 6-121 is covered by the copyright of this book.

Material from the following sources is acknowledged:

Lutheran Book of Worship and *Lutheran Book of Worship Ministers Edition*, ©1978 Lutheran Church in America, The American Lutheran Church, The Evangelical Lutheran Church of Canada, and The Lutheran Church-Missouri Synod.

Occasional Services, © 1982 Association of Evangelical Lutheran Churches, Lutheran Church in America, The American Lutheran Church, and The Evangelical Lutheran Church of Canada.

Book of Common Prayer (1979) of The Episcopal Church.

Prayers We Have in Common, © 1975 International Consultation on English Texts: the Apostles' and Nicene Creeds.

Praying Together, © 1988 English Language Liturgical Consultation: the Apostles' Creed, the Nicene Creed, the preface dialogue, the canticle texts "Lord, have mercy," "Glory to God in the highest," "Holy, holy, holy Lord," "Lamb of God," and "Now, Lord, you let your servant go in peace."

The Revised Common Lectionary, © 1992 Consultation on Common Texts.

New Revised Standard Version of the Bible, © 1989, Division of Christian Education of the National Council of Churches of Christ in the United States of America.

Composers of liturgical music are acknowledged: Daniel Kallman (b. 1956), Jeremy Young (b. 1948), Robert Buckley Farlee (b. 1950), and J. Bert Carlson (b. 1937).

Authors/translators of liturgical texts are acknowledged: Susan Palo Cherwien (b. 1953), Gail Ramshaw (b. 1947), Martin A. Seltz (b. 1951), and Frank Stoldt (b. 1958).

ELCA churchwide and publishing house staff: Norma Aamodt-Nelson, Ruth Allin, Lorraine Brugh, Carol Carver, M. Alexandra George, Lynette Johnson, Mary Ann Moller-Gunderson, Mark Junkert, Ellen Maly, Paul R. Nelson, Kristine Oberg, Rachel Riensche, Michael Rothaar, Ann M. P. Schroeder, Martin A. Seltz (co-editor), Frank Stoldt (co-editor), Samuel Torvend, Karen Ward.

Music engraving: A-R Editions, Inc., Madison, WI.

Indexes: Craig Mueller, Paul Schuessler.

Copyright and Permissions

Copyright acknowledgment: The publisher gratefully acknowledges all copyright holders who have granted permission to reproduce copyrighted materials in this book. Every effort has been made to determine the owner(s) and/or administrator(s) of each copyright and to secure needed permission. The publisher will, upon written notice, make the necessary correction(s) in subsequent printings.

Permission information: Permission to reproduce the service outline of Holy Communion, Setting 6 (pp. 42-45) for one-time use in weekly worship folders is hereby granted to any purchaser of this volume provided that no part of such reproduction is sold and the following credit line is used: Reprinted from *With One Voice,* copyright © 1995 Augsburg Fortress. Used by permission.

Permission to reproduce any other copyrighted words or music contained in this book must be obtained from the copyright holder(s) of that material. For addresses of copyright holders not listed on page 123 or for further copyright information, please contact Augsburg Fortress.

Copyright Holders and Administrators

ABINGDON PRESS (THE UNITED
METHODIST PUBLISHING HOUSE)
201 Eighth Ave. S., P.O. Box 801
Nashville, TN 37202
615/749-6422   FAX 615/749-6512

ARCHDIOCESE OF
PHILADELPHIA, Music Office
222 North 17th St.
Philadelphia, PA 19103-1299
215/587-3696   FAX 215/587-3561

ASIAN INSTITUTE FOR
LITURGY AND MUSIC
P.O. Box 3167
Manila 2800, Philippines
                  011-632-721-6140
          FAX 011-632-722-1490

AUGSBURG FORTRESS
426 S. 5th Street, P.O. Box 1209
Minneapolis, MN 55440
800/328-4648   FAX 612/330-3455

CHURCH HYMNAL CORPORATION
445 Fifth Avenue
New York, NY 10016
800/233-6602   FAX 212/779-3392

CONSULTATION ON COMMON
TEXTS/ENGLISH LANGUAGE
LITURGICAL CONSULTATION
1275 K Street NW
Washington, DC 20005-4097
202/347-0800   FAX 202/347-1839

COPYRIGHT COMPANY
40 Music Square East
Nashville, TN 37203
615/244-5588   FAX 615/244-5591

CPH PUBLISHING
3558 South Jefferson Ave.
St. Louis, MO 63118
800/325-0191   FAX 314/268-1329

DAVID HIGHAM ASSOCIATES
5-8 Lower John Street, Golden Square
London W1R 4HA, England
                  011-44-71-437-7888
          FAX 011-44-71-437-1072

GIA PUBLICATIONS
7404 South Mason Avenue
Chicago, IL 60638
708/496-3800   FAX 708/496-2130

HAL LEONARD CORPORATION
7777 W. Bluemound Rd.
P.O. Box 13819
Milwaukee, WI 53213
414/774-3630   FAX 414/774-8387

HINSHAW MUSIC, INC.
P.O. Box 470
Chapel Hill, NC 27514
919/933-1691   FAX 919/967-3399

HOPE PUBLISHING COMPANY
380 South Main Place
Carol Stream, IL 60188
800/323-1049   FAX 708/665-2552

INTEGRITY MUSIC
1000 Cody Road
Mobile, AL 36695
205/633-9000   FAX 205/633-5202

KEVIN MAYHEW LTD.
Rattlesden, Bury St. Edwards
Suffolk, IP3 0SZ England
                  011-44-973-7978
          FAX 011-44-973-7834

LITURGICAL PRESS, THE
Box 7500, Collegeville, MN 56321
612/363-2213   FAX 612/363-3299

LUTHERAN THEOLOGICAL
COLLEGE AT MAKUMIRA
c/o Augsburg Fortress

MORNINGSTAR MUSIC
2117 59th Street
St. Louis, MO 63110
800/647-2117   FAX 314/647-2777

NEW DAWN MUSIC
P.O. Box 13248
Portland, OR 97213
800/243-3296   FAX 503/282-3486

NEW GENERATION PUBLISHERS
John Ylvisaker
Box 321, Waverly, IA 50677
319/352-4396

NOVELLO AND COMPANY
8/9 Frith Street
London W1V 5TZ, England
                  011-44-71-434-0066
          FAX 011-44-71-287-6329

OCP PUBLICATIONS
5536 NE Hassalo
Portland, OR 97213
800/547-8992   FAX 503/282-3486

OXFORD UNIVERSITY PRESS
200 Madison Ave.
New York, NY 10016
212/679-7300   FAX 212/725-2972

OXFORD UNIVERSITY PRESS
3 Park Road
London NW1 6XN, England
                  011-44-71-724-7484
          FAX 011-41-71-723-5033

PILGRIM PRESS/
UNITED CHURCH PRESS
700 Prospect Ave. E
Cleveland, OH 44115-1100
216/736-3700   FAX 216/736-3703

RESOURCE PUBLICATIONS
160 E. Virginia St. #290
San Jose, CA 95112-5876
408/286-8505   FAX 408/287-8748

SELAH PUBLISHING COMPANY
58 Pearl Street, P.O. Box 3037
Kingston, NY 12401-0902
914/338-2816   FAX 914/338-2991

SPARROW CORPORATION
P.O. Box 5010
Brentwood, TN 37024-5010
615/371-6997   FAX 615/371-6800

WALTON MUSIC CORPORATION
170 NE 33rd St., P.O. Box 24330
Fort Lauderdale, FL 33307
305/563-1844   FAX 305/563-9006

WESTMINSTER JOHN KNOX PRESS
100 Witherspoon St.
Louisville, KY 40202-1396
502/569-5060   FAX 502/569-8090

WORLD COUNCIL OF CHURCHES
150 Route de Ferney
P.O. Box 2100
CH 1211 Geneva 2, Switzerland
                  011-41-22-791-6111
          FAX 011-41-22-798-1346

Topical Index of Hymns and Songs

673	I'm So Glad Jesus Lifted Me
781	My Life Flows On in Endless Song
726	Oh, Sing to God Above
795	Oh, Sing to the Lord
793	Shout for Joy Loud and Long

Judgment
629	All Earth Is Hopeful
627	My Lord, What a Morning
744	Soon and Very Soon

Justice *see Society*

Kingdom of God
764	Blest Are They
718	Here in This Place
740	Jesus, Remember Me
762	O Day of Peace
783	Seek Ye First the Kingdom of God
753	You Are the Seed

Last Times
745	Awake, O Sleeper
627	My Lord, What a Morning
762	O Day of Peace
691	Sing with All the Saints in Glory
744	Soon and Very Soon

LENT, 655-662
745	Awake, O Sleeper
732	Create in Me a Clean Heart
746	Day by Day
738	Healer of Our Every Ill
702	I Am the Bread of Life
739	In All Our Grief
713	Lord, Let My Heart Be Good Soil
769	Mothering God, You Gave Me Birth
695	O Blessed Spring
750	Oh, Praise the Gracious Power
733	Our Father, We Have Wandered
614	Praise to You, O Christ, Our Savior
734	Softly and Tenderly Jesus Is Calling
714	The Thirsty Fields Drink In the Rain
737	There Is a Balm in Gilead
741	Thy Holy Wings
785	Weary of All Trumpeting
716	Word of God, Come Down on Earth
779	You Who Dwell in the Shelter of the Lord

Light
652	Arise, Your Light Has Come!
776	Be Thou My Vision
729	Christ, Mighty Savior
800	Each Morning Brings Us
718	Here in This Place
649	I Want to Walk as a Child of the Light
630	Light One Candle to Watch for Messiah
728	O Light Whose Splendor Thrills
659	O Sun of Justice
651	Shine, Jesus, Shine

Love
664	A New Commandment
751	As Man and Woman We Were Made
666	Great God, Your Love Has Called Us
765	Jesu, Jesu, Fill Us with Your Love
680	O Spirit of Life
665	Ubi Caritas et Amor
749	When Love Is Found
716	Word of God, Come Down on Earth

Marriage
751	As Man and Woman We Were Made
748	Bind Us Together
648	Jesus, Come! For We Invite You
749	When Love Is Found

Maundy Thursday
664	A New Commandment
666	Great God, Your Love Has Called Us
765	Jesu, Jesu, Fill Us with Your Love
667	Stay Here
665	Ubi Caritas et Amor
663	When Twilight Comes

Mary, Mother of Our Lord
692	For All the Faithful Women
730	My Soul Proclaims Your Greatness
634	Sing of Mary, Pure and Lowly
632	The Angel Gabriel from Heaven Came

Ministry
652	Arise, Your Light Has Come!
760	For the Fruit of All Creation
719	God Is Here!
666	Great God, Your Love Has Called Us
752	I, the Lord of Sea and Sky
756	Lord, You Give the Great Commission

Mission *see Witness*

MORNING, 725-727
633	Awake, Awake, and Greet the New Morn
800	Each Morning Brings Us
771	Great Is Thy Faithfulness
777	In the Morning When I Rise
627	My Lord, What a Morning

Offertory *see Stewardship*
759	Accept, O Lord, the Gifts We Bring
705	As the Grains of Wheat
758	Come to Us, Creative Spirit
732	Create in Me a Clean Heart
703	Draw Us in the Spirit's Tether
760	For the Fruit of All Creation
708	Grains of Wheat
754	Let Us Talents and Tongues Employ
761	Now We Offer
710	One Bread, One Body
766	We Come to the Hungry Feast

Palm Sunday *see Sunday of the Passion*

Peace
757	Creating God, Your Fingers Trace
774	Dona Nobis Pacem
763	Let Justice Flow like Streams
781	My Life Flows On in Endless Song
762	O Day of Peace
750	Oh, Praise the Gracious Power
641	Peace Came to Earth
724	Shalom
766	We Come to the Hungry Feast
785	Weary of All Trumpeting
780	What a Fellowship, What a Joy Divine

PENTECOST, THE HOLY SPIRIT, 680-688
719	God Is Here!
775	Lord, Listen to Your Children Praying
756	Lord, You Give the Great Commission

PRAISE, ADORATION, 786-802
782	All My Hope on God Is Founded
671	Alleluia, Alleluia, Give Thanks
674	Alleluia! Jesus Is Risen!
699	Blessed Assurance
747	Christ Is Made the Sure Foundation
717	Come, All You People
758	Come to Us, Creative Spirit
640	Gloria *(Taizé)*
637	Gloria, Gloria, Gloria
719	God Is Here!
722	Hallelujah! We Sing Your Praises
720	In the Presence of Your People
631	Lift Up Your Heads, O Gates
730	My Soul Proclaims Your Greatness
726	Oh, Sing to God Above
635	Surely It Is God Who Saves Me

PRAYER, 772-775
740	Jesus, Remember Me
783	Seek Ye First the Kingdom of God
667	Stay Here

Reconciliation *see Forgiveness/Healing*
745	Awake, O Sleeper
735	God! When Human Bonds Are Broken
738	Healer of Our Every Ill
762	O Day of Peace
750	Oh, Praise the Gracious Power

Reformation Day
747	Christ Is Made the Sure Foundation
756	Lord, You Give the Great Commission
750	Oh, Praise the Gracious Power
755	We All Are One in Mission

Repentance *see Forgiveness/Healing*

Saints' Days
692	For All the Faithful Women
689	Rejoice in God's Saints
691	Sing with All the Saints in Glory

Scriptural Index of Hymns and Songs

Text and Music Sources

Tunes—Alphabetical

Tunes—Metrical

S M (Short Meter—6 6 8 6)
  CATECHUMEN 662
  FESTAL SONG 652
  ST. THOMAS 763
S M and refrain
  CHRISTPRAISE RAY 750
  VINEYARD HAVEN 631
C M (Common Meter—8 6 8 6)
  AZMON 745
  CHESTERFIELD 723
  DUNLAP'S CREEK 675
C M and refrain
  BICENTENNIAL 711
  GIFT OF FINEST WHEAT 711
  MANNION 679
  NJOO KWETU, ROHO MWEMA 687
C M D (Common Meter Double—8 6 8 6 8 6 8 6)
  FOREST GREEN 725
  KINGSFOLD 730
L M (Long Meter—8 8 8 8)
  ALL MORGEN IST GANZ FRISCH 800
  BERGLUND 695
  DUNEDIN 757
  ERHALT UNS, HERR 657
  JESU DULCIS MEMORIA 659
  NORWICH 769
  O WALY WALY 749
  PUER NOBIS 688
L M and refrain
  GAUDEAMUS DOMINO 658
  LINSTEAD 754
L M D (Long Meter Double—8 8 8 8 8 8 8 8)
  JERUSALEM 762
4 4 6 and refrain
  ONE BREAD, ONE BODY 710
4 5 10 4 5 10 and refrain
  EARTH AND ALL STARS 674
5 5 6 D
  HEAR MY PRAYER 772
5 5 8 D
  BUNESSAN 693
5 6 5 6 5 6 5 5
  CANTAD AL SEÑOR 795
5 6 5 6 5 6 7
  UYAI MOSE 717
6 4 6 4 and refrain
  NENO LAKE MUNGU 712
6 6 6 6 4 4 4 4
  LOVE UNKNOWN 661
6 6 6 6 and refrain
  PERSONENT HODIE 793
6 6 8 8 6 6 and refrain
  MARCHING TO ZION 742
6 6 9 6 6 9
  MIDDLEBURY 669
6 7 6 7 and refrain
  VRUECHTEN 676
6 7 6 8 D and refrain
  ROSAS 726
6 7 7 6 and refrain
  BIND US TOGETHER 748
6 8 7 7 and refrain
  BURLEIGH 627
7 6 7 6 and refrain
  ROYAL OAK 767
7 6 7 6 D
  BARONITA 692
  BRED DINA VIDA VINGAR 741
  DISTLER 785

HERZLICH TUT MICH VERLANGEN 733
  KING'S LYNN 647
  KUORTANE 755
  NYLAND 755
  PASSION CHORALE 733
7 7 7 4 and refrain
  GIVE ME JESUS 777
7 7 7 4 D and refrain
  HERE I AM, LORD 752
7 7 7 6
  GAYOM NI HIGAMI 727
7 7 7 7 and refrain
  LIVING GOD 700
7 7 8 8 9
  HUNGRY FEAST 766
7 7 9 and refrain
  CHEREPONI 765
7 8 7 7
  STAY WITH US 743
7 8 7 8 4
  ST. ALBINUS 653
7 8 7 8 8 8
  LIEBSTER JESU, WIR SIND HIER 716
8 4 8 4 8 8 8 4
  AR HYD Y NOS 721, 760
8 5 8 5 8 4 3
  CASTLEWOOD 758
8 5 8 5 and refrain
  GO DOWN, MOSES 670
  TUBMAN 670
8 5 9 5 and refrain
  STONERIDGE 706
8 6 8 8 6 6
  REPTON 768
8 7 8 7
  BARBARA ALLEN 759, 796
  BETH 683
  KAS DZIEDAJA 656
  MERTON 735
8 7 8 7 and refrain
  HANSON PLACE 690
  HOW CAN I KEEP FROM SINGING 781
  TE OFRECEMOS 761
8 7 8 7 D
  ABBOT'S LEIGH 719, 756
  BEACH SPRING 697
  JACKSON NEW 672
  JOYOUS LIGHT 638
  MISSISSIPPI 691
  RAQUEL 634, 635
8 7 8 7 3 3 7
  MICHAEL 782
8 7 8 7 6
  BRIDEGROOM 685
8 7 8 7 6 7 6 7
  GREENSLEEVES 701
8 7 8 7 7 7
  IRBY 643
8 7 8 7 8 7
  JULION 682
  NAGEL 655
  PRAISE, MY SOUL 654
  UNION SEMINARY 648, 703
  WESTMINSTER ABBEY 747
8 7 8 7 8 7 11
  OUIMETTE 698
8 7 9 8 8 7
  BESANÇON 626

First Lines and Common Titles

ISBN 0-8006-0138-8

136 | FIRST LINES AND COMMON TITLES